"Karen Johnson-Weiner has forged deep relationships with Amish folks across the country, attending weddings and work frolics, visiting one-room schools, and conversing around kitchen tables. In *All about the Amish*, she freely shares her expertise and insight. Authoritative and accessible, this book answers your questions thoughtfully and thoroughly."

—**Steven M. Nolt,** author of *A History of the Amish*

"Karen Johnson-Weiner ably and comprehensively presents answers to pervasive questions about Amish life based on her years of intimate research with the Amish. Her book is an accessible introduction to Amish culture and, at the same time, undoes the many barriers to Amish culture that have been created through myths, misunderstandings, and popular representations."

—**Joshua R. Brown,** professor of German and linguistics at the University of Wisconsin-Eau Claire and co-editor of *Pennsylvania Germans: An Interpretive Encyclopedia*

"Karen Johnson-Weiner is a superb guide to the perplexing questions of Amish life. Her keen wit entertains. Her sharp eye uncovers fascinating detail. A wealth of information and wisdom."

—**Donald B. Kraybill,** author of *The Riddle of Amish Culture*

"Karen Johnson-Weiner is far more than a student of the Amish. She is a tireless friend and advocate. Her writings consistently demonstrate a respect for the quiet dignity of this misunderstood culture, and the current question-and-answer format is no exception. Here, she tackles the enormous range of their beliefs and behaviors, selecting key elements to create an essential overview. The writing is concise and precise. She anticipates the most common questions, and offers answers in a compact format, all without sacrificing necessary information. The result? A book that draws on the depth and breadth of her knowledge to supply the reader with a keen understanding of who the Amish are, and how they live their lives. For anyone seeking a starting point to explain this Plain people, a quick reference guide, or a comprehensive refresher, this is the resource!"

—**James A. Cates,** clinical psychologist and author of *Serving the Amish: A Cultural Guide for Professionals*

"Professor Johnson-Weiner, a distinguished scholar in the field of Amish studies, has drawn on a wealth of knowledge to produce a book that provides readers with up-to-date and reliable information on one of America's most familiar yet often misunderstood groups. Written in a concise and refreshingly accessible way, this book will appeal to anyone who has ever been curious about who the Amish are and how they live out their faith in community."

—**Mark L. Louden,** Alfred L. Shoemaker, J. William Frey, and Don Yoder Professor of Germanic Linguistics and director of the Max Kade Institute for German-American Studies at the University of Wisconsin-Madison

all

ABOUT

the

AMISH

KAREN M. JOHNSON-WEINER

all

ABOUT

the

AMISH

Answers to Common Questions

HERALD
P R E S S

Harrisonburg, Virginia

Herald Press
PO Box 866, Harrisonburg, Virginia 22803
www.HeraldPress.com

Library of Congress Cataloging-in-Publication Data
Names: Johnson-Weiner, Karen, author.
Title: All about the Amish : answers to common questions / Karen M.
    Johnson-Weiner.
Description: Harrisonburg, Virginia : Herald Press, [2020] | Includes
    bibliographical references.
Identifiers: LCCN 2020000488 (print) | LCCN 2020000489 (ebook) | ISBN
    9781513806297 (paperback) | ISBN 9781513806310 (ebook)
Subjects: LCSH: Amish--United States--Social life and customs. |
    Amish--United States--Social conditions.
Classification: LCC E184.M45 J64 2020 (print) | LCC E184.M45 (ebook) |
    DDC 289.7/73--dc23
LC record available at https://lccn.loc.gov/2020000488
LC ebook record available at https://lccn.loc.gov/2020000489

ALL ABOUT THE AMISH
© 2020 by Herald Press, Harrisonburg, Virginia 22803. 800-245-7894.
    All rights reserved.
Library of Congress Control Number: 2020000488
International Standard Book Number: 978-1-5138-0629-7 (paperback),
    978-1-5138-0631-0 (ebook)
Printed in United States of America
Cover and interior design by Reuben Graham

Unless otherwise noted, Scripture quotations in this publication are from the *Holy Bible*, King James Version.

24 23 22 21 20   10 9 8 7 6 5 4 3 2 1

For Bruce

CONTENTS

Part 3

WHAT DOES IT MEAN TO BE "PLAIN"?

Part 4

WHAT IS IT LIKE TO GROW UP AMISH?

Part 5

WHAT ARE AMISH COURTSHIP AND WEDDINGS LIKE?

Part 6

WHAT IS LIFE LIKE FOR AMISH ADULTS?

Part 7

WHAT WILL AMISH LIFE BE LIKE IN THE FUTURE?

Part 1

WHO ARE THE AMISH?

Are the Amish Christian? Where do the Amish come from?

Who were the first Amish?

When did the Amish come to America? Are there still Amish in Europe?

What is the difference between Amish and Mennonite?

What does "Old Order Amish" mean?

Not all Amish look alike. Are there different kinds of Amish?

Where do the Amish live?

Are the Amish Christian? Where do the Amish come from?

The Amish are Christian. All Amish churches trace their roots to the Anabaptists, a radical offshoot of the Protestant reform movement that began in October 1517, when Martin Luther (1483–1546) challenged Pope Leo X by posting ninety-five theses about the sale of indulgences on the door of the Castle Church in Wittenberg, Germany, unwittingly launching the Protestant Reformation. Luther went on to argue that the Bible, not the church, should serve as the final authority on salvation, and that every Christian had the right to read and interpret the Bible. The Catholic church, in his opinion, needed reform. Yet, he trusted neither Catholic hierarchy nor lay people to undertake what he viewed as necessary changes, and therefore called on secular government to reform the church.

Many were ready for church reform. Thanks to Johannes Gutenberg's introduction of moveable type printing nearly a century earlier in Europe, people were reading the Bible in their own language for the first time, and numerous Bible study groups had formed, with some of them questioning for the first time church practices for which there seemed to be no scriptural justification. Some people wanted to get rid of any church practice that seemed to have no biblical basis.

In Zürich, Switzerland, the reform movement gained momentum with the election of a former Catholic priest, Ulrich Zwingli (1484 –1531), to be the city's head pastor. Many had hopes that Zwingli would move swiftly to remove statues from the church and abolish the priesthood. But Zwingli, like Luther, believed that civil authorities should direct change. He refused to carry out any reforms that had not been approved by the Zürich city council, which had assumed authority over all church activities. Zwingli's caution and the slow pace of reform angered several of Zwingli's students, notably Conrad Grebel (ca. 1498–1526), the son of a prominent Zürich family, and Felix Manz (ca. 1498–1527), a Zürich citizen. Grebel and Manz, along with Georg Cajacob, nicknamed "Blaurock" (ca. 1492–1529) argued that waiting on the Zürich city council to enact reforms meant that secular authority would outrank Scripture. In their eyes, the Bible should be the highest authority and basis for reforming the church.

The conflict came to a head over the issue of infant baptism. While the practice had religious significance, it also served to ensure that children were entered into state records. Effectively, on being baptized children became citizens of the state. Thus, infant baptism served both spiritual and secular purposes. Grebel, Manz, Blaurock, and others argued that the baptism of infants should have no place in church practice because it was not mentioned in the Bible. Instead, they asserted, baptism should serve as a sign of faith and commitment to the church.

When the Zürich city council enacted laws requiring the baptism of infants and outlawing any attempt to rebaptize those who had been baptized as infants, Grebel, Manz, and Blaurock broke with Zwingli and the state church. Meeting secretly in Zürich on January 21, 1525, the three rebaptized each other, launching the Swiss Brethren, a movement that became more popularly known as Anabaptist.[1] Theirs, they argued, would be a church of believers.

The Anabaptists wanted to establish a church that Christians could freely chose to join by expressing their faith through baptism. Consequently, the Anabaptists sought to separate the church from the authority and influence of the state. Unlike the Catholics, they were not interested in controlling the state, nor were they willing, like the newly formed Lutheran Church or the Zürich Church under Zwingli's guidance, to cede control of church matters to secular authorities. Hence, the Anabaptists posed a threat to established authorities and risked exile, torture, and even death. Early Anabaptist leaders paid dearly for their efforts at reform. Grebel was exiled and died at age twenty-seven; Manz was drowned in the Limat River, which flows through Zürich; Blaurock was burned at the stake.

In 1527, early Anabaptists convened in Schleitheim, Switzerland, and put their beliefs into writing in a document known as the Schleitheim Confession.[2] This document calls for individuals to join the church through voluntary baptism, for church members to reject violence and deal with those members who have sinned by banning them from fellowship, and for ministers to be chosen from the congregation through a lottery. The Schleitheim Confession also asserts that being Christian means obeying Christ's teachings in everyday life. Only in the church, a community of believers separate from secular, worldly society, could church members follow Christ's example. The goal was *Gelassenheit*, a complete surrender to God's authority and will.

In the sixteenth century, Menno Simons (1496-1561), a Dutch priest turned Anabaptist minister, was influential in shaping Anabaptist practice in western Europe, reinforcing an understanding of the church as a community, as a fellowship of believers rather than a building or a set of rituals. Living according to Christ's example and gathering together to worship, the church community would be separate from worldly society in doctrine, life, and worship. By the beginning of the seventeenth century, Anabaptists in western Europe had become known as Mennonites, followers of Menno.

Even early on, Mennonite practices varied regionally and culturally. While some Mennonites lived and practiced their faith in relative security, others faced persecution. One key difference related to the practice of excommunication. Menno

Simons argued that excommunication, called *Bann*, should be accompanied by *Meidung* or "shunning." For Simons, shunning meant avoiding the person who was banned in social situations as well as religious ones. In other words, church members would be prohibited from eating, drinking, doing business with, or engaging in any other social interaction with someone who had been excommunicated until that person repented and rejoined the church fellowship, a position called *streng Meidung* or "strong shunning." Others, however, disagreed, arguing that a banned person should only be shunned from taking communion (*kleiner Bann* or smaller shunning) or participating in other religious practices.

Mennonite leaders gathered in the Dutch town of Dordrecht in 1632 to iron out disagreements over church practice, including their divergent views of Bann and Meidung. Ultimately, Mennonite leaders upheld strong shunning as important because it both protected the church from sin and demonstrated to sinners the error of their ways, encouraging them to repent and rejoin the church community. The agreement they reached, called the Dordrecht Confession, further defined Anabaptist practice and became both a statement of Anabaptist belief and a guide to church practice.

The Dordrecht Confession was influential throughout the Mennonite world. Nevertheless, not all church leaders signed it, nor were all congregations eager to accept some of the practices it enshrined. For example, the Dordrecht Confession mandated foot washing as part of the communion ritual, something many Swiss Mennonite congregations did not do. More importantly, despite the decision reached on the importance of streng Meidung, many congregations continued to reject it. Some sixty years later, these differences led those who would become known as "Amish" to cease fellowshipping with the larger body of Mennonite churches.

Who were the first Amish?

Mennonites in Alsace and Lorraine in modern-day France were able to live relatively peaceful lives in the late 1600s. These Mennonites interacted socially with non-Mennonite neighbors and assimilated into non-Mennonite society. But such interaction with non-Mennonites concerned Jacob Ammann, a minister who worried that Mennonites were becoming lukewarm in their faith and too worldly in their lifestyle.

In 1693, Ammann called for reform, urging all congregations to adhere strictly to the Dordrecht Confession and be visibly separate from their worldly neighbors. When many ignored his call, Ammann summoned his followers to cease fellowshipping with them, dividing the Anabaptist world into Mennonite and "the Jakob Ammann group"[3] or the Amish.

Despite later attempts to reconcile, the split in the Mennonite church was permanent. Jacob Ammann's followers became known as the Amish. In the early days following this schism, the Amish also became known as the *Häftler* or "hook-and-eye people," because they chose to use this simpler means of fastening their clothing instead of buttons, which they considered more worldly. The Mennonites were called *Knöpfler* or "button people."[4]

When did the Amish come to America? Are there still Amish in Europe?

In response to religious persecution in Europe, many Amish immigrated to North America. They arrived in two broad waves.[5] Amish in the first wave (roughly 1717–1750) came mostly from Switzerland and the Palatinate region of

Germany. Attracted by William Penn's offer of land and religious tolerance, they settled primarily in what is now the state of Pennsylvania.

Amish who arrived in the second wave of immigration from Europe (roughly 1817–1861, came largely from the regions of Alsace and Lorraine in France. Seeking cheaper land, many of these Amish immigrants settled further west and north, establishing communities in Ohio, Illinois, Iowa, New York, and Ontario.

Today there are no Amish left in Europe. By the early twentieth century, the last remaining Amish congregations descended from those first established by followers of Jacob Ammann had rejoined the Mennonites.[6]

What is the difference between Amish and Mennonite?

Both the Amish and the Mennonites remain committed to a Bible-centered faith. Like their Anabaptist forebears, both groups believe in the voluntary nature of church membership and neither group practices infant baptism. Further, both Amish and Mennonites are committed to the separation of church and state. They remain pacifist, rejecting war as a way to solve political problems, and they view repentance and forgiveness as keys to following Christ's example. Both groups take to heart Christ's instruction to love their enemies.

But the Amish and the Mennonites have evolved differently. Today nearly 2 million Mennonites around the world meet weekly in church buildings or designated meetinghouses, with individual congregations joining with others to form conferences or associations of like-minded believers. Decisions about church matters are made at the conference level and enacted in individual congregations. The result is a very diverse Mennonite world.

Old Order Mennonites groups such as the Stauffer Mennonites and the Groffdale Conference, or "Wenger Mennonites," rely on horse-and-buggy transportation, speak Pennsylvania Dutch in the home and German in church services, and educate their children only through the eighth grade. The Old Order Weaverland Conference, or "Horning Mennonites," also retain distinctive dress and limit assimilation to worldly society but its members drive cars and use English in church services. Conservative Mennonites retain elements of plain dress, including prayer coverings for women, but they have adopted Sunday schools. More progressive Mennonite groups, such as Lancaster Mennonite Conference, Mennonite Church USA, and Mennonite Church Canada, have assimilated into mainstream society, founded colleges and universities, and been active in social justice issues and mission work.

Unlike the conferences that link Mennonite congregations, each Amish congregation or "church district" is independent and is led by ministers chosen from among the baptized men of that district. Because there is no hierarchical structure that links individual Amish congregations, there may be considerable variation from one Amish church district to the next, even when districts are geographically close to each other. Today groups calling themselves "Amish" retain plain dress, but they range from the ultraconservative Swartzentruber Amish, who will only ride in private cars if no public transportation is available, to car-owning-and-driving Beachy Amish. As this book shows, the Amish are diverse in their dress, their use of language, and the *Ordnungs* by which they live their faith.

What does "Old Order Amish" mean?

The majority of Amish are called simply "Old Order," a term that goes back to the mid-nineteenth century. At that time, there were a number of small, scattered Amish church communities in North America. Some were established by the first Amish arrivals from Germany in the early part of the eighteenth century. Others were started more than a century later by immigrants from the Alsace and Lorraine regions of modern-day France.

Problems arose among the Amish in North America because the newer church communities, shaped by a different history and regional European culture, tended to be more innovative. These later arrivals were "already of a different view in church matters than the former immigrants of about a hundred years before," as one Amish writer described.[7] The later immigrants were more tolerant of worldly dress, had differing views on important issues such as baptism and education, and were impressed and influenced by mainstream Protestant practices such as prayer meetings and Sunday schools.

By the mid-nineteenth century, with Amish settlements functioning in relative isolation from each other and each settlement facing varying hardships, differences in practice were established that threatened the unity of the Amish world. A number of ministers met in small, regional meetings and attempted to establish consensus on important Anabaptist practices, including separation from the world, excommunication and shunning, and pacifism and nonresistance. Eventually, however, growing tensions between conservative and progressive communities began to reach a breaking point. In 1862, the first of a series of annual ministers' meetings was held in Wayne County, Ohio. Although the majority of participants were from Ohio, the meetings were open to all Amish and

attended by a variety of church leaders from different states.[8]
Those who gathered hoped that an open discussion of their
differences would help them standardize religious practices
and ensure church unity once and for all.

At first, participants seemed to find the unity they were
looking for. For example, they were united in their opposition
to military service and posing for photographs. Nevertheless,
deep divisions remained, and after 1865 the most conservative ministers stopped attending this annual meeting. Perhaps
the meetings were doomed to fail, for the progressive faction had a very different notion of what the meetings were
supposed to accomplish than their conservative counterparts. The differences stemmed from their understandings of
Ordnung, the church discipline that defined the boundaries
of church practice for the congregation. Progressive Amish
leaders wanted a fluid set of guidelines that would evolve
through ongoing meetings that brought together Amish
church leadership. They envisioned church leadership being
united to hand down guidelines and set practices for the
individual congregations. Their conservative counterparts
wanted to keep the Ordnung as a fixed set of regulations
set and maintained by each individual congregation. This
conservative understanding of Ordnung reinforces the independence of each congregation and the boundaries between
the church community and outsiders.

There was no reconciling these different positions. Although
the ministers' meetings continued until 1878, the conservative
faction had ceased attending several years earlier. Eventually,
those who maintained a more traditional understanding of the
Ordnung became known as the *Alte Ordnung* or Old Order
Amish, and their church communities became marked by their
desire to continue with as little change as possible to the practices of daily life and religious observance. The majority of the

more progressive Amish communities eventually formed several regional conferences, each of which eventually rejoined their Mennonite brethren.

Not all Amish look alike. Are there different kinds of Amish?

Today there are about forty different Amish affiliations, or groups of congregations. The groups that share similar Ordnungs are more likely to cooperate with each other. Some are known by the names of past bishops: the Swartzentruber Amish, the Troyer Amish, the Beachy Amish. Others are known by quirks of history. For example, the Nebraska Amish do not come from Nebraska but at one time the bishop guiding the group did.

In other words, the Amish are hardly the unchanging representatives of bygone days that popular culture might have us believe. In fact, since the first Amish arrived in North America, the Amish have been changing in response to political necessity, new circumstances, and personal challenges. And like those first Amish arrivals, today's Old Order Amish continue to draw on tradition and Scripture to define themselves in a changing world. Lacking any central organizing structure that would unite all congregations, each Amish church is a distinct and self-defined community, separate not only from the non-Amish community that surrounds it, but also from most other Amish ones as well. This means that the church community decides, by itself, what its Ordnung, or rules of the church, will be. And since no two congregations have faced exactly the same combination of historical, personal, regional, social, and economic factors, there are a variety of differences, some quite subtle (e.g., some groups will not use LED flashlights) and some obvious (brown buggies versus black, gray, or white ones). A church community may *dien* or "fellowship" with others whose Ordnungs are similar, meaning that ministers from one group are able to preach in church services held by the others and that a member of one church community might marry a member of one of the others. Although a church community may consult with those with which it fellowships, it must ultimately find its own path.

There are, however, concrete reasons why groups differ. Sometimes distance causes difference. For example, in the early twentieth century, in response to moves by school officials in Lancaster County, Pennsylvania, to close one-room schoolhouses and send rural children to large central schools, a number of Amish families left Lancaster for St. Mary's County, Maryland. In the first years after the move, the buggies, dress, and other customs of the St. Mary's families remained the same as those of the families who stayed in Lancaster, but over the years, the small, subtle changes occurring in both groups began to add up. Nearly a century later, the buggies used by the descendants of those who moved are noticeably different from those of their Lancaster cousins. A buggy in Lowville, New York, a community that traces its roots to that move from Lancaster to Maryland, is gray, like its Lancaster counterpart. Unlike the Lancaster buggy, however, the Lowville buggy does not have a windshield.

Other differences have come from economic and social changes in mainstream society. For example, as mainstream farmers have expanded their acreage and mechanized production, Amish farmers, particularly in the larger, older settlements, have struggled with growing populations and increasingly limited access to good, affordable farmland. In response, some Amish communities have permitted wage labor in non-Amish workplaces, and young people in some Midwestern Amish communities now work in factories instead of on farms. In other settlements, children now routinely work with their parents, not on family farms, but in family businesses that may also employ others from the community. Still other groups, wanting to keep their agriculturally based way of life, have moved in search of affordable farmland, establishing new Amish communities in regions such as Maine, Vermont, and Prince Edward Island, Canada, which had never before seen Amish settlement.

Importantly, change affects social relationships within the community, creating a diversity in the Amish world that is most apparent in the way different Amish groups have accepted or rejected the technology of mainstream society. The Old Order Amish continue to reject automobile ownership and public grid electricity. Nevertheless, solar power, computers, and cell phones are increasingly evident in a number of Amish settlements. While some communities still harvest ice and store perishables in cool cellars and ice chests during the hot summer months, others employ propane gas to power stoves and refrigerators, which means that they still do not need to connect to the grid to enjoy the benefits of these appliances. All Amish use batteries to power flashlights, but many Amish also use them for a variety of small devices, such as clocks and calculators. Others use them to run power tools and cash registers.

But change does not always come easily, and as each Amish church community decides for itself what accommodations it will make, not only to mainstream society, but also to changes occurring in other Amish communities, there can be conflict. For example, following the ministers' meetings in the nineteenth century, Old Order Amish congregations had to decide what to do with church members who left the church in which they'd been baptized. While there was no doubt that those who left the Amish to join a Catholic or mainstream Protestant church should be excommunicated and shunned, many Amish church communities were conflicted about what to do with those who left to join one of the growing number of more progressive Amish or Mennonite churches that retained plain dress and traditional worship but seemed to allow a more assimilated lifestyle.

More conservative Amish argued that those who joined a congregation with an Ordnung that differed from the one they had promised to uphold at baptism had broken their baptismal vow and should be excommunicated and socially shunned. This position, called streng Meidung or strong shunning, was rejected by many fellow church members. Unable to reconcile the disparate positions, church communities divided into separate groups. In 1910, Amish in Lancaster County, Pennsylvania, who were opposed to streng Meidung withdrew from the Old Order to establish a new church. Called the Peachey Amish by their neighbors, this group soon adopted more mainstream Protestant practices, such as Sunday school, and embraced many of the technological innovations, including the telephone, that were beginning to challenge Old Order groups. In 1927, the Somerset County, Pennsylvania, Old Order community divided when Bishop Moses Beachy rejected streng Meidung. Beachy's followers became known as the Beachy Amish, and by 1930 had adopted the use of both automobiles and electricity but retained distinctive clothing.

More recently, the New Order Amish, which formed in 1966, decided that farmers may use tractors in the field, but they still forbid automobile ownership. In contrast to their Old Order counterparts who express the hope of salvation but refuse to say that they "know" they are saved because only

God can know, the New Order Amish emphasize the personal assurance of salvation, a more individualistic understanding of the believer's relationship to God.

Schisms have also resulted in far more conservative groups, such as the Swartzentruber Amish, the Nebraska Amish, and the Troyer Amish, all of whom have drawn a sharp line between the church community and mainstream society and have restricted the use of all but the most limited technology. For example, arguing for streng Meidung, the Swartzentruber Amish divided from the Old Order Amish in Holmes County, Ohio, in the early part of the twentieth century. Since then, the Swartzentruber churches have faced internal struggles, and there are now several different kinds of Swartzentruber groups, but all continue to reject the use of motorized vehicles and electricity, upholstered furniture and linoleum, chain saws, and hydraulic power. They also put strict limits on employment in the non-Amish world.

Such splits are evidence of the ongoing Amish struggle to follow Christ's example and live according to Anabaptist principles in the face of pressure, both from the dominant, non-Amish society and from forces within the group. The result is a diverse Amish world, marked by variations in everything from dress to education to the use of technology.

Where do the Amish live?

In 1900, there were approximately 5,000 Amish people living in North America, with communities in thirteen states and the province of Ontario. Since then, the Amish population has skyrocketed, and new communities have been established in states far from the earliest Amish settlements, including Maine, Texas, and Montana. Today there are close to 350,000 Amish in communities spread across 31 states. Nearly 6,000 more Amish live in Canada, which now has Amish communities not only in Ontario but also in Prince Edward Island, Manitoba, and New Brunswick. Most recently, Amish communities have been established in Argentina and Bolivia, which together have a combined Amish population of approximately 200.

The states with the largest Amish populations are Pennsylvania and Ohio, followed closely by Indiana, Wisconsin, and New York (in that order). With an Amish population of over 5,500, Ontario boasts the largest number of Canadian Amish communities.[9]

Part 2

WHAT ARE AMISH CHURCH COMMUNITIES LIKE?

What is the Amish church? Where do they worship?

How are Amish communities organized?

What happens if there is disagreement within a community?

How does someone become an Amish minister or bishop?

When do the Amish get baptized? What is baptism like in an Amish community?

Can anyone join the Amish?

What happens if someone leaves the Amish?

What is the Amish church? Where do they worship?

Like their Anabaptist ancestors, who worshiped in secret by hiding in barns or in private homes to conduct their services, today's Amish do not meet in church buildings. Every other Sunday, they gather for worship in the home of one of the families in the congregation. Each family takes its turn to host church and to provide the fellowship meal that follows the service. For the Amish, "church" is much more than a Sunday service.

The standard German word for church is *Kirche*. Like its English equivalent, *Kirche* refers to the building in which worship services are held or to the services themselves. However, the word for church in Pennsylvania Dutch (also called Pennsylvania German[1]), the language spoken in Amish communities, is *Gmay*, from the German *Gemeinde*, meaning community. For the Amish, the church is not the building in which they meet or even the worship services themselves. Rather, the church is a community formed by those dedicated to putting the teachings of Christ into practice. It is the one pervasive force in Amish existence. The *Gmay* is separate from the world because, according to Amish belief, God's people must be separate from the world "that [they] may be blameless and harmless, the sons of God, without rebuke" (Philippians 2:15).

As asserted in the Schleitheim and Dordrecht Confessions and reinforced by centuries of persecution, the Amish believe that the Christian way will not be chosen by the majority of society, and thus, they remain "a peculiar people" (Titus 2:14), separate from the world and prepared to suffer at its hands.

How are Amish communities organized?

The most important social unit in Amish communities is the family. The family may even be seen as the Amish church in microcosm, for its formal structure reflects the structure of the church community, which itself is the larger family of those who gather to put Christ's teachings into practice.

Amish fathers guide their families, just as the ministers guide the church, reading Scripture in the morning when the family rises and again before they retire for the night. The father sits at the head of the table with his wife at his side, and the children sit in order of age, boys on one side and girls on the other. This seating pattern is reflected in the seating at church services too, where men sit together on one side and women on the other, with boys and girls in their own places. Each child knows his or her place in an Amish family and in the community.

The size of a church district or congregation is measured by the number of families who regularly gather for worship, not by the number of individuals at the service. The key events of the church community—church services, weddings, and funerals—all take place in the context of the family home.

Amish families join in worship with other families in their church district. Church districts, the equivalent of "congregations," include all the families living within a particular geographic area. Generally including twenty to forty families, church districts vary in geographic size depending both on the number of families and the distance they must travel. In particularly dense Amish settlements, for example, a district may be geographically quite small and church members might walk to services. In rural settlements, Amish families may find themselves traveling several miles by horse and buggy to attend church services.

When districts get too crowded, they divide, creating two districts of relatively equal size. Each new district then goes on independently, although the two resulting districts continue to fellowship with each other. Amish people attend church services in the district where they live, although they may visit church services in other districts.

Each church district is led by a three-part ministry. There is a deacon (in German *Armen-Diener* or "minister to the poor"), whose responsibilities include assisting in marriage arrangements and seeing that the material needs of all in the community are met. Two to three preachers (*Diener zum Buch* or "minister of the book") are responsible for preaching and counseling. Finally, there is a bishop (*Voelliger-Diener* or "minister with full powers"[2]), who performs marriages, baptisms, excommunications, and funerals. All church members, meaning all those who have joined the church by becoming baptized, take part in church decision-making, and decisions about the Ordnung and church matters are made within and by the congregation itself.

As in the earliest Anabaptist churches, each Amish district or church congregation has its own Ordnung, which has evolved over time as the group has responded to changing circumstances. Some changes in the Ordnung may contribute to the economic viability of a community, such as when a district decided to accept the use of bulk milk tanks when the market for canned milk disappeared.[3] Other changes are reactions to legislation and social changes in the dominant society, such as decisions to accept (or reject) the use of slow-moving vehicle signs on buggies or the decision to start private schools in the face of public school consolidation. Because no two communities have faced the same set of circumstances, no two Amish congregations have exactly the same Ordnung. Even when there is general agreement, the results might be quite diverse. For example, all Old Order Amish forbid automobile ownership, but buggy styles vary from group to group, as do the rules governing when one can accept rides in cars from non-Amish neighbors.

Ordnungs are reaffirmed twice each year, in the spring and in the fall, at *Ordnungsgmay*, or council church. At Ordnungs-gmay, church leaders express their views on the Ordnung, comment on practices that are forbidden or discouraged, and remind church members of past decisions. After this, each member of the church is asked whether he or she is in agreement. In what John A. Hostetler characterized as a "cleansing ritual," differences of opinion must be ironed out and consensus reached.[4]

By creating norms with which all agree, the Ordnung ties the community together. It is a *Zaun*, a fence, against the outside world and obedience to it is a symbol of love for the church.[5] In the end, if there is consensus and all are in agreement, the community can celebrate *Grossgmay* or church communion at its next worship service two weeks later.

Ordnungs help to shape patterns of interaction in the Amish world. A congregation may *dien* or "fellowship" with others whose Ordnungs are similar. This means that ministers from one group are able to preach in church services held by the others, and that a member of one congregation might marry a member of one of the others.

Church districts linked by spiritual bonds or historical and social connections form affiliations. The most conservative affiliations have put the strictest limitations on technology use within the community, while more progressive affiliations demonstrate more varied interaction with mainstream society, even permitting church members to work in non-Amish businesses or use cell phones for their own businesses. Yet even within such affiliations, each congregation must ultimately find its own path.

What happens if there is disagreement within a community?

When disagreements about church practice or Ordnung divide church members, the congregation cannot observe and celebrate communion, which normally takes place at a special service every spring and every fall. This is a difficult time for all. To help resolve the difficulties, the church community may choose to call on ministers from other church communities with which the group fellowships. These outside ministers will talk with each faction and attempt to achieve a consensus. If differences cannot be resolved, the community will split.

Not all disagreements within the church community are the same, however. For a conflict to be recognized as a schism, each side must have a minister or bishop. At this level of disagreement, with ministers on both sides of the argument, the two factions recognize a sincere difference of opinion that is beyond their ability to settle. In the weeks immediately following the schism, while each of the different factions regroups, church members may move freely from one group to another, an open window to personal change that closes only when each group holds its first worship service as a separate entity. Because one party to the schism does not shun the other, such splits provide relief for tensions that may have been building over a long period and allow smaller, more unified groups to emerge.

Regardless of the reason for disagreement, a split in a church district is about identity and how members of the group will be distinguished from nonmembers. This is a matter of utmost importance for a people whose religious beliefs call on them to remain separate from the world.

Schism within a church district divides families and ruptures work and social ties. During one split, for example, one Amish woman compared the emotional turmoil to that suffered by a divorcing couple. Nevertheless, schisms are evidence of the ongoing struggle by the Amish to apply Anabaptist principles in the face of pressure, both from non-Amish society and from forces within the group.

How does someone become an Amish minister or bishop?

Only baptized Amish men can be ordained to the ministry. Each community is likely to want for a minister a man who is married with a family, someone who has demonstrated that he is a stable member of the church community, someone committed to the Ordnung and the traditions with which he was raised. This is important because, while the church community leaves the final choice of minister in God's hands, each baptized church member is involved in the selection.

When a district needs a new deacon or minister, church members nominate likely candidates. Both men and women nominate candidates, and those receiving a particular number of nominations, depending on the community, are placed "in the lot." Those in the lot retire to a side room while copies of the *Ausbund*, the Amish hymnbook, are laid out on a bench. One of the hymnbooks contains a slip of paper with a Bible verse on it. As the candidates come out one at a time, each picks up a hymnbook. God is understood to make the final choice, for the new minister will be the one who picks up the hymnbook with the slip of paper. Bishops are chosen by lot from the group of those already ordained.

Amish men do not seek to become ministers. Indeed, any man who campaigned for the role would likely be seen as unacceptable by the rest of the community. Ministers serve an unpaid, lifetime appointment. They take on the onerous duties of guiding their church community spiritually in addition to their other work. Being in the lot is stressful, even for those who are not chosen, and wives breathe a sigh of relief if the lot does not fall to their husbands.

Because God has chosen a particular person to be a minister, other church members should listen closely to what he says. But ministers should not be dictatorial. Rather, the community runs for the most part through consensus and compromise and the shared commitment of church members to the Ordnung.

When do the Amish get baptized? What is baptism like in an Amish community?

Despite growing up in Amish families, being nurtured by their parents and grandparents in the values of their church community, and taking part in nearly all aspects of Amish life, Amish children are not church members. They become so only when they are baptized. To become baptized or not is a decision Amish young folk generally make in their late teens or early twenties. It is not one that young people take lightly, for baptism is a vow to God and a lifetime commitment to the church community and its Ordnung. Those who are considered too young or unready to take on the responsibilities of church membership may be counseled to put off baptism.

Typically, young people who have made the decision to "join church" meet with their ministers in the spring to prepare for the step they are about to take. Although baptismal instruction varies from community to community, the would-be church members typically go over the articles of the Dordrecht Confession. The Dordrecht Confession defines the church as a community of those committed to separation from worldly ways and builds into daily life a commitment to tradition. It embodies the understanding that Christ's church is eternal, God's truth is eternal and unchanging, and those who follow God's path must not be influenced by secular fads or changing styles. Importantly, young people preparing for baptism are reminded of the seriousness of the step they are about to take, and young men are also reminded that by taking the baptismal vow they are agreeing to serve in the ministry should they ever be chosen to do so.

The Amish have a hope of salvation but do not believe, as Catholics and some others do, that baptism "saves" them. In becoming baptized, young people acknowledge their faith in Jesus Christ, renounce worldly ways, and vow to support the Ordnung of their church community. Baptism is a commitment to God that shapes a host of other choices: whether and who to marry, where and how to live, what kind of work to do. Individuals become church members through baptism, and should they leave the church or violate their baptismal vows, they will be put in Bann (excommunicated) and Meidung (shunned).

The baptismal ceremony itself comes after the second of two sermons that are part of the Amish church service. Candidates for baptism are questioned about their willingness to take this step and then remain kneeling before the congregation as the bishop offers a baptismal prayer. Following the prayer, the deacon pours a small amount of water into the bishop's cupped hands as he holds them over the head of each baptismal candidate, baptizing each in the name of the Father, Son, and Holy

Ghost. After this, the new church members are welcomed into the congregation with a handshake and a kiss of peace.

Baptismal church is generally held in the spring, and it is followed two weeks later by Ordnungsgmay, or council church, at which time all baptized church members meet to reaffirm their commitment to the Ordnung of their church community. Two weeks later, at *Grossgmay*, members celebrate the unity of the church community with communion. As they celebrate communion for the first time, the newly baptized young people take on the rights and responsibilities of church members.

Can anyone join the Amish?

There have been converts to the Amish, although not very many. Many of those who wish to convert are drawn by what they see as a simpler or more stable lifestyle, while others turn to the Amish to reject modern society or to express a yearning for a particular kind of religious experience.

According to researchers, about half of converts are family groups and the rest are predominantly single men. Also, some communities attract more converts than others.[6] Fewer than half of those who convert to the Amish remain as part of an Amish community, which suggests how difficult the transition to Amish life can be. To become a full participant in an Amish church community, baptism may be only the start. One needs to take on a new language, a new lifestyle, new patterns of dress, and perhaps most difficult of all, a new way of interacting with others.

In joining the Amish, one joins a community that prizes consensus over individual desire. Many who join have followed an individual longing to leave mainstream society behind. For some, it is then difficult to suppress self and individual desires in favor of group unity.

What happens if someone leaves the Amish?

Roughly 85 percent of Amish young people choose to become baptized in their church communities. The percentage is higher in more conservative communities. Those who choose not to be baptized have little role as adults in the church community, and most drift away. They disappoint their parents, who hope that at some point the young person finds his or her way back to the church community. However, having never joined the church, those who elect not to be baptized are not subject to shunning.

If a young person chooses to be baptized and then, at some point in the future, violates the Ordnung or leaves the church community, he or she is judged to have broken a sacred baptismal vow and will face Bann (excommunication) and Meidung (shunning). Excommunication and shunning are acts of "tough love," an attempt to persuade errant church members to see the errors of their ways and return to the fold. "When we ban someone out of church, we turn it over to the Lord and let the Lord take over," said one Amish church member.[7] "It's the last love we can show for them, to try to get them back." While shunning one's own children seems particularly harsh to those who are not Amish, Amish parents have little choice. They have taken their own baptismal vows, which they would violate by not shunning those who have willfully placed themselves outside of the church community.

What excommunication and shunning mean in daily life varies from one church community to another. At one extreme are Amish church communities that practice streng Meidung, the strongest form of shunning. In such communities, there will be little to no social interaction of any kind with someone who is "in Bann." In other communities, those who have been baptized can leave more easily. Although in Bann, they may interact with families but just not eat at the same table with baptized church members or help in the preparation of food or other chores. One ex-Amish woman noted that those in her community could not accept gifts from her, nor could she offer them rides in her car or give them money. Further, she could not purchase things from them and could not sit with church members at the same table for meals. Nevertheless, she was permitted to attend funerals in the community, and she continued to interact with her siblings.

For Amish parents, having a child leave the church community means losing that child to the world. Parents worry about the child's future, not just in this life but the next. While parents are obligated to "train up a child in the way he should go" (Proverbs 22:6), children are biblically commanded to "honour thy father and thy mother" (Exodus 20:12).[8] Many Amish take a child's decision to leave the church as not just a violation of the commandment but as a personal rejection of parental teachings.

Whether or not a young person decides to leave the Amish can be affected by several factors, including the father's occupation, family issues, affiliation, and schooling. Some Amish young people leave and return several times before either leaving for good or settling down in their Amish community.[9] Importantly, those who leave the Amish before being baptized often leave for different reasons than those who leave after joining church, often with a spouse and children.[10] When young folk leave, they may do so because they see more social and economic opportunity outside the church community. They may also be fleeing dysfunctional families, perhaps the victims of abuse.[11] Surveying those who left the Amish, Charles E. Hurst and David L. McConnell found that most of those who left the large Holmes County area settlement did so either for a less restricted lifestyle or to have a "more intense religious experience."[12]

Part 3

WHAT DOES IT MEAN TO BE "PLAIN"?

Why are the Amish called the "Plain People"?

Plain means "without adornment" or "not fancy." For the Amish and other Plain groups, such as Old Order Mennonites and Hutterites, to be plain also means to be simple, humble, and removed from the consumerism of the non-Plain world. Plain is used to describe the descendants of the first Anabaptists who, in their distinctive dress, transportation, lifestyle, and use of language, have drawn a visible line between themselves and those in mainstream society.

What language do the Amish speak?

Most Amish children learn to speak Pennsylvania Dutch (also called Pennsylvania German) as their first language. Pennsylvania Dutch, a dialect of German or *Deutsch*, is an unwritten, unstandardized language. Its use as the language of conversation within the church community helps to keep the group separate from English-speaking society. Transmitted orally, Pennsylvania Dutch varies from region to region, from one community to another. Some Amish communities use a dialect variant called Swiss.

While the Amish converse with other Amish in Pennsylvania Dutch, Amish folks use English to interact with those outside the Amish community. In fact, the Amish refer to non-Amish as the "English."[1] But although *spoken* English represents the outside world, *written* English plays an integral role in Amish life. For the Amish, English is also the language of reading and writing, and it serves as the primary language of instruction in

Amish schools. Amish magazines and Amish newspapers, *The Budget* and *Die Botschaft*, are all published in English.

In religious services, the Amish also use "church German." This is an archaic form of German used in their religious books, including the Bible and their hymnal, the *Ausbund*. Beginning in the third grade, Amish children start learning to read the old *Fraktur* script (a sixteenth-century German typeface) so that they can read the hymnbook and the Bible in this form of German.

Why don't the Amish use electricity?

The Amish are marked by their willingness to do without electricity and other technology that most people in mainstream society could not imagine living without. To understand this, however, it is important to look beyond individual technologies like electricity and focus on how the Amish see themselves in relationship to mainstream society or "the world." Like their Anabaptist forebears, today's Amish consciously attempt to live "not conformed to the world" (Romans 12:2). The Bible says, "Love not the world, neither the things that are in the world" (1 John 2:15). The Amish interpret this as an admonishment about not loving the values of mainstream society, along with its vices and fads, and the technologies that would lead church members to assimilate to it. They believe that God's people must be a faithful minority, "strangers and pilgrims" (1 Peter 2:11) living in the world but not being integrated into mainstream society. The Amish interpret the command to be separate from the world literally. In refusing to assimilate to "English" or non–Old Order society, they put strict barriers between themselves and the outside world. Thus, church community Ordnungs limit the use of particular technologies.

When electricity first began to appear in rural areas, the Amish decided that connecting to the public grid would link Amish homes with the world and harm the church community. The Amish did not think that electricity itself was bad; rather, they came to the conclusion that electricity in Amish homes would permit the adoption of other technology that would change their way of life, promote greater individualism, and weaken the church community's influence. By rejecting public grid electricity, the Amish were able to keep a host of other technological innovations, including television, out of Amish homes.

Even as they rejected public grid electricity, however, the Amish have made use of electricity from other sources. All Amish use batteries, for example. While the most conservative use them only for flashlights, other Amish use batteries to power various things, including buggy lights, calculators, clocks, household lamps, electric shavers, and even photocopying machines. Other Amish use solar power to run a variety of household items, including appliances, word processors, and electric fences. In some communities, Amish farmers have put solar panels on top of carriage houses to recharge the batteries that power the lights on their buggies. In fact, there are even Amish entrepreneurs who market solar power installations to non-Amish clients as well as to fellow church members.

The Amish have long been aware of how technology can disrupt daily face-to-face interactions that reinforce personal ties and strengthen church community bonds. They know, for example, that the labor-saving devices so important in many modern households eliminate the need for people to work together to accomplish tasks. A dishwasher, for example, means it no longer takes two people to clean up after a meal, one to wash the dishes and another to dry them. (No Amish communities permit dishwashers.) As the Amish see it, fewer chores mean fewer opportunities for family members of all ages to work together and enjoy the companionship of shared labor.

When confronting new technology or technological innovation, the Amish are guided by tradition and Ordnung. The whole community decides whether something is acceptable. Decisions made by the church membership and incorporated into the Ordnung become binding upon subsequent generations, who respect the faith in which previous decisions were made and see in the process a heavenly endorsement.[2] This does not mean that the Amish will keep an outdated tool just because their grandparents used it. It does mean, however, that they will not rush to get the newest version of that tool just because it is the newest version. The Amish consider how new technology will affect their church communities and act accordingly. If there is a sense that it will have little impact, then an innovation may become widespread with little notice. Yet even the smallest innovation might cause internal dissension. Among the ultraconservative Swartzentruber Amish, for example, subgroups can be distinguished by their acceptance or rejection of LED flashlights.

Because each Amish church community decides for itself where to draw the line and what technology to exclude, the Amish world is diverse. Some districts allow propane gas appliances but others do not. Some districts allow indoor flush toilets and stationary bathtubs with running water but others do not. Some districts allow chainsaws but others reject them.

Sometimes it is not a simple matter of acceptance or rejection. Some communities adapt a particular technology to fit within Ordnung guidelines, rendering it suitable for church members to own. For example, in many communities small gasoline motors are used to operate sewing machines and washing machines. Some communities permit kerosene-powered refrigerators and freezers. In other settlements, farm machinery designed to be pulled and powered by tractors is fitted with gas motors and pulled by horses. In progressive Amish settlements, one can even find battery- or solar-powered calculators, cash registers, and word processors.

The Amish have also been at the forefront of invention, creating systems designed specifically for nonelectric homes. For example, Amish inventors successfully modified propane-powered lamps so that they could run off the same gas source as refrigerators and freezers. Thanks to this innovation, families in Amish communities that permit the use of propane no longer have to have separate propane tanks for each lamp.[3]

Why do Amish ride in cars but refuse to own them?

With the automobile, as with electricity, the Amish have taken an approach that privileges face-to-face, local interaction that strengthens church community bonds. More specifically, they have drawn a sharp distinction between "owning" technology, which risks letting it control one's lifestyle, and "using" technology, which keeps one in charge.

In the early twentieth century, as private ownership of automobiles became widespread, the Amish saw in the automobile an obvious threat to their way of life. Automobiles can quickly take their owners far beyond the boundaries of the church community, away from home and neighbors. Further, the automobile puts travel at the convenience of its owner, privileging the individual over family and group. Most importantly, the car culture of mainstream America serves as a reminder of a worldly way of thinking that the Amish reject. As many church members point out, someone who leaves the church will likely buy a car as soon as possible.

The Amish see nothing wrong with the technology of the automobile. Having always used public transportation, including trains, ferries, and buses, they simply treat the automobile as another type of public transportation. It has been forbidden to own cars but not to use them.

Many Amish churches allow members to hire a private car and driver for long-distance travel. Again, the most conservative groups have the greatest restrictions. The Swartzentruber Amish will not hire drivers, nor will they accept rides when there is public transportation available. Even when a neighbor or close friend provides transportation in an emergency, such as a trip to the hospital, the Swartzentruber Amish attempt to reimburse them for their time and gas. After all, if one can have a car ride any time, then one will start using it when it is not necessary, and the car, not the church community, will be in control.

This difference between "owning" and "using" and the emphasis on maintaining social ties between family members and others in the church community are also evident in the Amish approach to the telephone. When the telephone was first introduced, for example, the Amish saw that it would not only bring the outside world into their home but also weaken the bonds created by face-to-face conversation. Further, ringing telephones would disrupt the household as answering the phone took priority over other activities and phone conversations between two people shut out conversation with others at each end of the line.

The Amish have always used phones, though. In the past, parameters to ensure that phones did not disrupt home and community life have kept them outside the house in sheds or small phone shanties in some communities. In other communities, Amish have had to rely on pay phones or phones belonging to obliging non-Amish neighbors. Nowadays, more progressive Amish may sanction the limited use of mobile phones or allow landlines to be in a business office only, while the most conservative Amish prefer not to speak on the phone and instead are likely to ask a willing non-Amish person to make a call on their behalf.

Are there special Amish foods? How do they preserve things without refrigerators?

There are no religiously prescribed Amish foods. Nevertheless, the Germanic origins of the Amish are reflected in meals featuring potatoes, meat, sausage, and slaw. Amish housewives are adept at making the recipes with which they grew up. After all, Amish women learn to cook by working with their mothers, so it is not surprising that recipes are handed down through the generations. (There are certainly Amish men who cook, but generally the Amish consider the kitchen to be the domain of women.)

After worshiping in each other's homes, Amish families stay to share a meal together. This meal is provided by the family hosting the service. Among some conservative groups, such as the Swartzentruber Amish and the Nebraska Amish, church members eat bean soup, bread and butter, homemade peanut butter spread (made with peanut butter and Karo syrup), and "church spread" (a spread made with marshmallow cream and flavored gelatin). In other communities, the menu may differ. Typically there will be bread and butter, cheese, church spreads, pickles, and pies, along with plenty of coffee. Schnitz pies are a common feature of Sunday fellowship meals. These pies, with a filling of dried apples or "schnitz," are often made as turnovers to be easily picked up and eaten.

Meals served at Amish weddings and other community events also vary from one type of church community to another. Importantly, the menu always reflects the traditions of each community. While there may be individual touches, it is community tradition that shapes special meals.

To preserve food, the Amish have traditionally canned or dried it. For farming families, this has reinforced the cyclical nature of Amish life. In the spring, families wait eagerly for strawberries and the other early produce (radishes, lettuce). Later, they gather and can a variety of vegetables and fruits, waiting until winter cold makes it possible to preserve freshly butchered meat until it can be processed.

Women in the most conservative Amish homes are more likely to work with others to preserve food. Generally, a mother is assisted by her unmarried daughters (or her sons, if she has no daughters at home). Sometimes the whole family gets involved. For example, when there are bushels of peaches to can, father and sons help mother and daughters to peel them all (just as mother and daughters help the male members of the family with milking and corn husking). Larger tasks, such as preserving home-butchered beef and pork by canning or smoking it, may require even more help. Often Amish families, groups of neighbors, or parents with married children take turns helping each other.

As some Amish move off the farm and establish larger family businesses or work for non-Amish employers, families produce less of their own food. A regular paycheck, for example, allows Amish housewives to shop for meat and other products and preserve them much the way their non-Amish counterparts do.

Relying on gas or kerosene refrigeration in some Amish communities has allowed a growing number of Amish housewives to preserve meat and produce by freezing it, a less labor-intensive process. Because Amish wives with access to freezers do not need as much help to can and preserve, they are more likely to work alone than their more conservative counterparts.[4]

Do the Amish pay taxes?

As law-abiding citizens, the Amish pay taxes. As it says in the Dordrecht Confession (see part 1), Christians should "faithfully pay the government custom, tax and tribute, thus give it what is its due, as Jesus Christ taught, did Himself, and commanded His followers to do."[5] The Amish also cite Matthew 22:21, in which Jesus says, "Render therefore unto Caesar the things which are Caesar's; and unto God the things that are God's."

Nevertheless, the Amish in the United States have objected to paying Social Security taxes on the grounds that it is the responsibility of family and church community, not the government, to take care of those in need. They cite 1 Timothy 5:8, which asserts that "if any provide not for his own, and specially for those of his own house, he hath denied the faith, and is worse than an infidel."

The Amish take seriously their responsibility to provide help and support to all those in the church community who need it. If a member of the community falls ill or a barn burns, the community will come together to donate labor, money, and spiritual and social support. The church community is there to provide care and support for those who are widowed or orphaned. They refuse to let a secular authority take over these obligations.

In 1965, changes to the Social Security Act Amendments exempted religious groups from contributing to the Social Security system if they provide for dependent members. In 1988, Congress exempted Amish employers from the requirement that they collect wage taxes from their Amish employees. Amish who work for non-Amish employers must still pay Social Security tax, even though many refuse to take the benefits to which they are entitled.

Do the Amish vote?

Although the Amish pay all other taxes and respect local, state, and federal authorities, they generally do not vote. However, this is not because Ordnungs forbid voting. Rather, most Amish feel that voting would make them part of secular authority rather than simply subject to it.[6] As one Amish guidebook puts it, "By voting, we become a part of the powers instead of being subject to them." In response to those who argue that the Amish could accomplish good things by voting, the same guidebook argues that "Christians have no business in politics. To suppose so is human reasoning. Getting involved in politics is stepping out of the role to which God has called us. It is the same as saying, 'Let us do evil, that good may come' (Romans 3:8)."[7] Those Amish who do vote are more likely to do so in local elections than in national ones.

The Amish stance on voting and taxes reflects their embrace of a "two kingdoms" theology, a belief that God has established both earthly secular governments to maintain order on earth and an everlasting kingdom in heaven. The Amish recognize the need to respect and obey secular, worldly authorities established by God. Yet they place their loyalty and duty in God's authority and God's everlasting kingdom first, rejecting any attempt by secular authorities to assume the functions of conscience or to exert control over the spiritual realm. If earthly authorities demand actions that bring the Amish into conflict with the church and God's authority, then the Amish respectfully refuse to comply. An Amish church member's first loyalty must always be to God.

This means that the Amish have often been caught up in conflict when the laws of the state or country are incompatible with Ordnungs. When this happens, the Amish generally try to work with authorities to find a suitable compromise. For example, the Old Order Amish Steering Committee emerged in the 1960s to negotiate farm deferments for young Amish men subject to the military draft. Although the committee (which today includes a "committee man" from each state with an Amish population) represents diverse Amish communities and cannot, in any way, be said to speak for the church, it does help negotiate the Amish response to secular bureaucracy.

In dealing with secular authority, particularly in cases that result in lawsuits or otherwise involve the court system, the Amish are often helped by outsiders. For example, the 1972 U.S. Supreme Court Case of *Wisconsin v. Yoder et al.* was carried out with the help of the Reverend William C. Lindholm and his organization, the National Committee for Amish

Religious Freedom. This case led to a ruling that states could not force the Amish to send their children to high school because it was in violation of Amish religious beliefs. Similarly, when ultraconservative Swartzentruber Amish in northern New York ran afoul of local building codes, the Becket Fund for Religious Liberty stepped in to represent them. These organizations received no payment for their work on behalf of their Amish clients. Although individual Amish may rely on the services of a public defender, if the practices of a church community are challenged by local authorities and no compromise is possible, members are likely to relocate rather than change their Ordnungs.

Why do Amish men have beards but no mustaches?

Amish men grow beards but shave their mustaches as another way to remain unconformed to the world. The Amish believe that God expects men to grow beards because he created them to do so. The Amish generally do not trim their beards, for, as it says in Leviticus 19:27, "Ye shall not round the corners of your heads, neither shalt thou mar the corners of thy beard." The wearing of beards has been part of Amish practice since Jacob Ammann led his followers in a schism from the larger Mennonite population (see part 1). Ammann argued that men should not trim their beards, which was a worldly fashion.[8] Ammann's male followers became known as *Bartmänner* or "beardmen."[9] Shaving the moustache off likely came later as a response to flamboyant military styles of the eighteenth century, in which the moustache was often curled or worn alone.

Today, when a young man actually starts to let his beard grow depends on the Ordnung of his church community. In some groups, men simply let the beard grow when it comes. In others, men wait to let their beard grow until they marry.

The untrimmed beard and lack of moustache serve as powerful symbols of identity, distinguishing the Amish from not only their worldly neighbors but also other plain groups. For example, Beachy Amish men trim their beards and Old Order Mennonite men generally shave them off.

The Amish also regulate hairstyles. For example, some church communities require the hair of boys and men to be cut "bowl style" (as if a bowl was put on the head and whatever hair stuck out was trimmed off). Others favor the "Dutch boy" or "window" cut, with the bangs cut shorter than the sides and back. The more conservative the church community, the longer men's hair is likely to be. Nevertheless, men's hair cannot be too long. After all, as it says in 1 Corinthians 11:14, "Doth not even nature itself teach you, that, if a man have long hair, it is a shame unto him?"

In contrast, Amish girls and women never cut their hair, for the next verse adds, "But if a woman has long hair, it is a glory to her: for her hair is given her for a covering" (1 Corinthians 11:15). Amish girls and woman cannot let their hair down. But as with beard growing, each Amish community has its own way of following the Scripture. While young girls in some communities wear their hair in buns in the back, girls in other communities have their hair braided in a design unique and traditional to their particular Amish church community.

Who tells the Amish how to dress, and why do they dress that way?

Ordnungs, the set of rules that govern each church community, define how the Amish dress. This means that clothing styles differ from one church community to another. As a result, Amish clothing styles, like Amish hair, play a powerful symbolic role. What an Amish person wears indicates not only an Amish identity as a Christian not conformed to the world, but also an identity as a member of a particular Amish community.

The style of clothing also indicates both age and gender. In short, one can look at an Amish person and know what type of Amish world he or she lives in and the role that person plays in the church community. For example, infant boys and infant girls often wear identical dresses. When a young boy is a year old or toilet trained (depending on the community), he begins to wear broadfall trousers (with a large flap in the front) and suspenders just like his father's. A young girl will continue to wear a dress but not one like her mother's. A young girl's dress will button in the back, and she will wear a pinafore apron over it. Only when her particular community considers her old enough will she wear more adult clothing, with a "front-shut" dress, a cape, and an apron around her waist.

The Amish do not consider their dress to be "Christian." Rather, as Christians, they feel that they should remain separate from worldly society. Their clothing should reflect this by being modest, humble, and in keeping with the Ordnung of the church community. Further, the Amish believe that complying with the dress standards of the church community shows a person's commitment to the church, while deviation reflects rebelliousness and worldliness.

Centuries ago, the Amish did not dress much differently than their non-Amish neighbors. Yet from the earliest days of the Amish movement, clothing helped distinguish the Amish from other Anabaptists. For example, Jacob Ammann emphasized conformity in dress among church members and was attentive to the sumptuary laws then in effect that mandated plain clothing.[10] Fewer than ten years after the schism between the Amish and the Mennonites, one Alsatian priest noted that Amish men had long beards and "the men and women wear clothing made only of linen cloth, summer and winter." In contrast, just a decade later the Mennonites had shorter beards and dressed "about like the Catholics."[11]

Over time, while the rest of the world adopted ready-made clothing and began to pay attention to seasonal changes in fashion, the Amish maintained their plain dress. Each element of clothing became subject to group consensus. When the Amish dress themselves each day, they signal both a religious and group identity.

There are some commonalities in Amish dress. While styles vary from one church community to another, every Amish female wears a prayer covering or "cap." In some communities, even infant girls wear a cap, but in others, girls begin to wear the covering every day only as they approach their teens. Generally, unmarried girls wear black caps and married women wear white ones. In some Amish church communities, though, unmarried girls in their teens begin to wear white caps for everyday use and black ones for church services. And in others older, unmarried women may decide to adopt the white cap for church as a sign, perhaps, that they no longer expect to marry. Bonnets are worn over caps, and bonnet styles, like cap styles, vary from one church community to another.

All Amish females wear an apron, a sign of willingness to work hard. They also wear capes, an item of clothing that originated in the scarf or kerchief worn around the neck by European women centuries ago. Finally, they wear dresses made from solid-colored fabric. Each of these items varies across Amish communities. For example, the length and color of women's dresses is set by each local Ordnung. Women in more conservative communities generally wear longer and darker-colored dresses than women in more progressive ones.

Men wear straw hats in summer and heavy felt hats with brims in winter. The style of the hats and the width of the brims are fixed in the Ordnung of each church community. More conservative communities require wider hat brims than more progressive ones. Ministers wear hats with wider brims than other men in the same church community. In some but not all Amish church communities, boys can wear knitted hats or toques during the winter.

Because of their distinctive dress, one Amish person can easily identify another and assess quickly what kind of community that person comes from. More importantly, when they get dressed in the morning, each Amish person reidentifies with the church community, reinforcing faith and community boundaries.

Do the Amish go to doctors?

The Amish are not opposed to modern medicine, and all Amish make use of mainstream medical care while also being guided by religious beliefs. It's not uncommon for Amish people to consult medical specialists in addition to using vitamins and homeopathic cures. Above all, they place their faith in the will of God.

Yet, as has become clear, there is diversity in the Amish world over actual practices. Simply because one Amish group does or accepts something does not mean another will. For example, the Swartzentruber Amish refuse to consider open heart surgery but those in other Amish groups accept the procedure.

In making decisions about healthcare, the Amish are guided by their own experiences along with those of friends and family. They feel most comfortable with a healthcare provider who is willing to listen to them, who will take their concerns seriously, and who is willing to respect their religious beliefs. They are most comfortable in an easygoing, low-tech environment, where they will not be rushed. Because they have only limited education—the Amish only go to school through the eighth grade—and likely do not speak English as their first language, they are often intimidated by the fast-paced, high-tech, jargon-filled world of modern hospitals.

The expense of medical care further constrains Amish interaction with mainstream medical providers. For religious reasons, the Amish do not have health insurance, although those employed by non-Amish businesses may participate in company healthcare plans. The Amish are exempt from the Affordable Care Act in the United States. As a result, they are aware of healthcare costs. They know that a trip to the emergency room or a visit with a specialist is likely to cost hundreds of dollars, and that any tests ordered may send the bill skyrocketing into the thousands. As a result, they are less likely to visit doctors for routine checkups or preventive care.

In the Amish world, it is believed that God provides. Viewing the body as a natural organism, the Amish see the importance of treating it with the remedies God provides. They understand chiropractic treatments, for a chiropractor works with the body alone. Similarly, they are drawn to natural remedies or cures based on plants that God has provided.

In contrast, the Amish often see in modern medical practice a rather arrogant human attempt to control the body, produce healthy outcomes, and even prolong life. While the majority of non-Amish patients would embrace these goals, many Amish see them as an attempt to thwart the will of God. After all, the Amish say, death is a natural prelude to life everlasting, and they find aggressive attempts to postpone the inevitable unwelcome.

This does not mean the Amish are fatalistic. If they were, they would never see a doctor. Like their mainstream counterparts, Amish people want to be healthy and avoid sickness and injury, and so they do consult healthcare providers. They use vitamins and homeopathic remedies, take prescription drugs, and have high-tech surgeries. But in general, they are more willing to stop a medical intervention or to not intervene at all because they accept God's will.

Given Amish religious beliefs, their reliance on community, and the expense of modern medical care, it is not surprising that the Amish draw on the resources of tradition and the wisdom of past generations. Why should an expectant mother go to an impersonal hospital when she can draw on the practical knowledge of an older woman in the community who has long served as a midwife? A neighboring midwife will come to the family home, understand what will make the new mother comfortable, and provide care in keeping with community expectations. The older generation also knows which teas will help with everyday ailments and can make herbal salves to help with skin ailments or minor burns.

The more conservative the Amish group, the more likely they are to turn to folk resources. In some ultraconservative communities, individuals are known for their ability to "draw pain," to lay their hands on an afflicted person and ease their suffering. This practice brings great comfort to those who are suffering and reinforces a sense of solidarity among community members.

Some Amish healers are quite well-known beyond their own church communities. Although they lack certification and accept donations instead of charging for their services (to get around laws governing medical practice), their patients are generally quite satisfied with the care they receive. For the Amish, turning to such folk practitioners makes sense. After all, the Amish believe, who better to go to when one is ill than someone who has experienced the same illness and found relief? Further, it is much easier to believe a relative or friend who shares your faith than it is to believe a doctor who does not know you—a doctor who wants you to take a drug with a name you cannot pronounce that is manufactured by a pharmaceutical company that wants to make money.

The Amish supplement the care they receive from doctors, hospitals, and folk practitioners with care they receive from family and friends. Caring for other members of the community is central to Amish identity, and church members see it as their Christian duty to care for the sick, the elderly, and the disabled. When someone falls ill or is injured, family members and members in the local church district also stand ready to offer care.

Amish people make regular visits to those who are injured, ill, elderly, or grieving. The informal network of Amish support is always ready to reach out with cards, letters, and visits to let those suffering and their families know that they are not alone. Sometimes the youth or young married couples sing favorite songs for the elderly or those confined to their home. People who are dealing with a particular illness make a special effort to reach out to those in similar circumstances. Parents who have lost a child will be sure to visit other parents similarly bereaved.

The Amish church community is there for its members in other ways as well. For example, when there is a new baby, a funeral, fire, or accident, people help by dropping off meals, doing chores, and running errands, Adult children may set up a weekly rotation to assist an elderly parent who needs constant care. Periodic countywide or regional gatherings for people with a certain disability or disease are also an important source of support that stretches beyond the family circle. Finally, financial support from family, church community, and friends is also typical, especially to pay high medical bills that would overwhelm a single family.

And when the end comes for someone, that person is never alone, and those who remain have company in their grief.

Part 4

WHAT IS IT LIKE TO GROW UP AMISH?

Do Amish children go to school?

All Amish children go to school through the eighth grade. In the United States, this was the norm for most children, whether Amish or not, prior to World War II. Until the mid-twentieth century, Amish children often attended small one-room public schools with their non-Amish peers. However, the public school system in the United States began to change at that time. Districts began to consolidate one-room schools into larger, centralized educational campuses, requiring rural children to travel farther away from family and community to attend classes. They also began to add new subjects to the curriculum, including physical education and music, which small one-room schools could not afford to offer. At the same time, states began to increase both the length of the school year and the number of years of compulsory education.

Amish parents resisted these changes. They refused to allow their children to be bused to centralized schools or go beyond the eighth grade. The Amish began to establish private schools within their own church communities when the mainstream schools began to change. The first Old Order private school was the Apple Grove Mennonite Private School in Dover, Delaware, founded in 1925. By 1957, there were 59 Old Order Amish schools in ten states and in the province of Ontario. By 1982, there were 130 Amish schools in Ohio alone.[1] Today there are too many Amish schools to count. By establishing their own schools, the Amish were able to control how and what their children were learning.

As the number of Old Order private schools grew, many Amish parents were fined or jailed for their refusal to obey the new public school requirements. The conflict between Amish parents and secular authorities was finally resolved in 1972, when the U.S. Supreme Court ruled in the case of *Wisconsin v. Yoder* "that enforcement of the State's requirement of compulsory formal education after the eighth grade would gravely endanger if not destroy the free exercise of [. . . Amish] religious beliefs."[2] After that, the number of small one- to three-room Amish schools grew, and building a schoolhouse has become one of the first tasks for settlers in a new community. There are no Amish high schools.

Amish schools reflect the values of the church communities in which they are located. In the most conservative settlements, schoolhouses are plain, typically one-room structures with no electricity, indoor plumbing, or playground equipment. Children learn to read and write English, to read the archaic German and Fraktur script of their German Bibles and hymnbooks, and to do arithmetic. They are usually taught by a young teacher, who is likely female and probably graduated from the eighth grade only a year or two before. Teachers receive no special training.

In the most progressive church communities, the schools may have two or three classrooms, indoor plumbing, and playgrounds featuring swings, basketball hoops, and other equipment. Children will likely study health, geography, social studies, and art, in addition to English reading and writing, German reading, and arithmetic. Their teachers are often older, some having chosen to make teaching a career, and teachers gather regularly to share ideas about pedagogy.

Amish schools do not offer instrumental music, home economics, calculus, computer programming, chemistry, or biology. Some Amish children, usually in more progressive Amish communities, do attend public schools until the eighth grade. There they are exposed to some of the subjects excluded from Amish school curriculums. In addition, some parents enroll children with special needs in public school special education classes.

Gertrude Enders Huntington points out that the "Amish do not confuse schooling with the larger concept of what the world calls education. Although during most periods in their history they have permitted their children to be schooled by 'outsiders,' they have never permitted their children to be educated by the world."[3]

For the Amish, schooling or book learning gives children the knowledge needed to interact with mainstream society in ways their church communities deem appropriate. In contrast, education—the true education upon which the church community depends for its survival—is the knowledge gained in sharing labor, worshiping together, and enjoying family and friends at home, in church, and in visiting. Education is what one learns within the community—enabling full participation as a church member, and being a good Amish parent. Education begins when the child is born and continues long after schooling is over.

What do the Amish like to read?

When Amish children start school, they first begin to learn to read and write in English. Although they will also learn German and the Fraktur script so that they can read the *Ausbund* and the German Bible, the Amish do most of their reading and writing in English.

While the Amish have access to all the same reading materials as their non-Amish counterparts, there are some newspapers, magazines, and books of particular interest to the Amish.[4] One of two weekly Amish newspapers is likely to be found in every Amish home. *The Budget*, published in Sugarcreek, Ohio, and

Die Botschaft, published in Millersburg, Pennsylvania, present letters from "scribes" in Old Order settlements rather than news of current political events or the latest fashions. These scribes write letters about what is happening in their home communities. The average letter will talk about where church was held, where it will be held next, any visitors to the community, births and deaths, and maybe offer a story about what the scribe or a neighbor has been doing. There is no negative gossip, nor is there any reporting about events within the community that only church members should know about. There is a seasonal timelessness to this "news," and Amish readers can keep up with what is going on in other communities, content in the knowledge that life is going on as it should.

A number of monthly periodicals are also widely read in Amish homes. Like the newspapers, *The Diary* offers reports from community scribes and has special sections reporting births, deaths, and marriages. It also offers updates on those who move from one church community to another. *Plain Interests* offers articles about farming, health, history, and other topics of interest to Old Order families. The Amish publishing company, Pathway Publishers, produces three monthly magazines: *Family Life* (a general interest magazine), *Young Companion* (aimed at teens and young unmarried Amish readers), and *Blackboard Bulletin* (a magazine for teachers and parents of schoolchildren).

The Amish also have some special-interest magazines, from *Life's Special Sunbeams*, a magazine for parents of children with special needs, to *The Little Red Hen News* and *Ladies' Journal*, two women's magazines that feature short stories and articles on food preservation and health. There are magazines for children (*Rainbows and Sunshine*), single women (*The Single Girls Newsletter*), Amish businesses (*Plain Communities Business Exchange*), and general interest (*The Connection*).

The Amish also read a wide variety of books and novels. Pathway Publishers produces books not only for Old Order schools, but also a variety of books aimed at readers of different ages. The Amish also appreciate books by Mennonite presses, including Herald Press. They often read literature from decades past, by authors such as Louisa May Alcott, Lucy Maud Montgomery, and Charles Dickens, perhaps because it reflects a way of life without telephones and televisions and an era when men and women play very different social roles. Many Amish also read Amish-themed romance novels. Linda Byler, one of the most popular authors of such fiction, is herself Amish. Finally, the Amish also like historical works, books about animals and farming, cookbooks, and other how-to books of practical knowledge.

What is an Amish church service like?

Held every other Sunday at a church member's home, the Amish church service usually lasts about three hours and is conducted in German. At each church service, the congregation is told where the next church service will be held. Because families "take church" in rotation, most members know when their turn will come. Although family events—a birth, a death—can affect the rotation, families plan ahead.

Once a family "gets church," they work hard for two weeks to ensure that their home will be ready to welcome the congregation. The entire house is cleaned, new shelf paper laid, pots and pans scrubbed, and walls and windows washed. Neighboring women and married daughters generally come to help mothers get ready. Meanwhile, fathers and sons will clean the yard and mow the lawn (usually with nonmotorized push lawn mowers). If they are a farming family, the stables will be cleaned, and the barns swept out.

During warm weather, the family might hold services outside in a shed. Otherwise, all furniture will be moved out of the home's main floor so that there is room to set up the benches, which must be transported, sometimes in what is called a church wagon, from the last place services were held. By Saturday evening, the family will have the benches all arranged for church the next morning.

Sunday morning begins early both for the family hosting church and for families who may have to travel some distance, either on foot or by horse and buggy. When a family arrives at a home for church services, mothers go into the house with any babies or little children. Older girls find their counterparts in the kitchen, washhouse, or woodshed, and boys find the other boys. After taking care of the horses, fathers gather in the yard to talk until it is time for the service.

Gender, marital status, and age determine how worshippers gather for the service. The ministers and bishop take their seats first, followed by the married men, with the oldest entering first. Married women, who have already been in the house for a while, take their seats on the opposite side of the house. Next, young unmarried girls enter single file, with the oldest, baptized girls leading the line. Finally, unmarried men enter, again with the oldest, baptized ones taking their places first.

Amish homes are generally built with a large kitchen and living room side by side on the first floor. Normally women and girls sit in the kitchen, and men and boys sit in the living room. The ministers sit in the front of the room in front of the men. However, this gender division is not absolute, and there may be several rows of unmarried girls behind the rows of unmarried men. Ministers stand to preach in the doorway connecting the two rooms so that all can hear. The congregation sits on backless benches, but the oldest members of the church community may be given regular chairs.

The rituals of coming in for church, hanging up hats, and finding a seat vary slightly from one church community to another, but the service is similar from group to group. After all are seated, the congregation sings several hymns from the *Ausbund*, a German-language hymnbook used among the Amish for more than four hundred years. An older man acting as *Vorsinger*, or song leader, announces the number of the hymn and begins each line as the rest of the congregation joins in. Any baptized man can be a Vorsinger, but it will usually be someone who has had some training. After the first hymn, the ministers and bishop withdraw, oldest first, to another room for the *Abrot* or counsel. During the Abrot, the ministers decide who will preach the sermons.

The second hymn at an Amish church service is always *Das Lobleid*, number 131 in the *Ausbund*. Because the Amish sing very slowly, this song may take up to half an hour to sing. The congregation continues to sing until the ministers return. Then they wait while the ministers take their seats. After all are seated, one minister rises to stand at the doorway between the rooms to preach the *Anfang*, or introductory sermon. After the Anfang, the congregation kneels for silent prayer, and then stands while the Deacon reads a chapter from the Bible. This first reading is followed by *Es schwere Deel* or the main sermon, and then another Bible chapter is read aloud.

After this second reading, other ministers or men in the congregation give *Zeugnis* or testimony in response to the main sermon. During this time, the minister who has preached invites his fellow church members to mention what he might have forgotten or to correct any mistakes he has made. Ministers have been chosen by lot and do not write their sermons.

Instead, they speak by inspiration, and their message comes from God and the heart.

After the testimonies, the minister who preached the main sermon thanks his fellow church members for their contribution, reminds the congregation that all praise is due to God, and invites the congregation to kneel for the final prayer. The congregation then stands for the benediction.

Following the benediction, the deacon announces where the next church service will be held, there is a closing hymn, and the service ends.

After the service, benches are turned into tables and the congregation shares a fellowship meal. Members of the congregation take their places at the table in much the same order as they entered the service itself, and women and men sit separately. There is much visiting after the meal, until everyone begins to head for home mid-afternoon. Unmarried young people will gather again in the evening for singing. Some may simply stay at the hosts' home if they're not needed at home for chores.

Every spring and fall there are extended services. First is *Taufsgmay* or the baptismal church, followed two weeks later by Ordnungsgmay or council church, and then two weeks after that, *Grossgmay* or the communion church service. Those who are not yet baptized take no part in these extended services, which last all day.[5]

Why don't Amish dolls have faces?

When the Amish make their own dolls, they do not draw or sew on faces. In the most conservative groups, they do not add arms or legs.

There are many explanations for why Amish dolls do not have faces. One is that this emphasizes how all are alike in God's eyes. Another is that the facelessness is in keeping with the commandment not to make graven images. Yet another is that adding the face would make the doll seem worldly and thus be a source of sinful pride.

Depending on the church community, however, Amish children may play with a variety of commercial dolls or stuffed toys, all of which have faces.

Why don't the Amish allow photos?

Another iconic characteristic of the Amish is their unwillingness to be photographed. The Amish have been averse to photographic portraits since photography became mainstream in the mid-nineteenth century. They view photographs as a violation of the commandment against making graven images (Exodus 20:4). Further, the Amish feel that posing for pictures demonstrates vanity, something the Amish discourage. All Amish groups forbid church members from taking photographs of others or posing for pictures.

What do the Amish do for fun? What are frolics?

The Amish do many of the same things for fun as their non-Amish neighbors. Little children swing, play with toys, and play house or school or otherwise mimic their parents. Older children play board games, volleyball, basketball, and softball. The Amish do not encourage competitive team sports, but teachers often group schoolchildren into teams for a good softball game, making sure that even the smallest first grader has a role to play. In some church communities, the young folk—young people aged sixteen or seventeen up to marriage—come together for picnics and other outings. In all church communities, the young people gather for singings in the evening on a church Sunday, with young men escorting their dates home afterward.

Importantly, the Amish do not draw the same line between work and play as their non-Amish counterparts. Little children learn by doing. This means they participate with parents and older and younger siblings in a variety of tasks. For Amish children, every chore can be a game. Pushing a manual lawnmower can be hard work. But it is much more fun if one sibling, tugging on a rope tied to the mower, pretends to be the horse and another, pushing from behind, pretends to be the driver. Amish games reflect the chores children do and the daily activities of their lives.

The Amish find pleasure in working together. A frolic is a gathering of friends and family to accomplish a task that a single person or family could not do alone. For example, when a couple wants to build a new house or a barn, they invite neighbors and family to help them. While the men and older boys dig the foundation and build the structure, the women and girls prepare a large meal, make snacks, wash dishes, and perhaps finish a quilt or two. Little children join in by playing, helping, running errands, and longing for the days when they can work like their older siblings and parents.

As the name "frolic" suggests, the event is a happy one. Not only does a considerable amount of work get done, but there is also good food, lots of conversation, joking, and friendship.

What holidays do the Amish celebrate?

The Amish celebrate the holidays of the Christian calendar: Christmas, Good Friday, Easter, Easter Monday, Pentecost, Pentecost Monday, and Ascension Day. Some groups celebrate a second day of Christmas, December 26. Many midwestern Amish groups also celebrate "Old Christmas" or Epiphany (Three Kings Day) on January 6.

Unlike their non-Amish neighbors, the Amish do not celebrate Christmas with bright lights or Christmas trees, nor do Amish children receive lots of gifts. Parents and grandparents are likely to give children clothes or practical items. Dating couples give each other small tokens, such as homemade greeting cards or handcrafted wooden boxes. In school, children color holiday pictures and give their teachers presents, and teachers are likely to give the schoolchildren candy and other small gifts. Many Amish families make candy, cookies, or other treats for the holiday, and they gather together to celebrate at a holiday meal. There may or may not be a church service, depending on the day of the week and when Christmas occurs in the service cycle. In a number of Amish communities, Old Christmas is a day of fasting.

Most Amish treat Good Friday as a day for fasting and prayer, and Easter is emphasized in church. While Amish schoolchildren may color pictures of Easter eggs and Easter bunnies and eat jelly beans, there are generally no Easter baskets at home.

Second Christmas, Easter Monday, Pentecost Monday, and Ascension Day are prime days for visiting. Among the most conservative groups, Easter Monday and Pentecost Monday are also considered good days for fishing. In some church communities, Ascension Day is a "half fasting day," meaning that church members go without breakfast, but others celebrate it as another fishing or visiting day.

Secular holidays celebrated by non-Amish neighbors generally pass with little fanfare in Amish communities. Amish families may gather for Thanksgiving but many say that every day is for giving thanks. New Year's Day is a time for needing new calendars but not celebrated in any special way. Independence Day, Memorial Day, and Labor Day pass unnoticed (except for the lack of mail delivery). Halloween is also not observed, although schoolchildren may color pictures of pumpkins and eat candy in school. Valentine's Day is a day for dating couples to give each other cards and gifts, and schoolchildren delight in making and passing out valentines and eating candy hearts. Depending on the family, children may also give their parents cards on Father's Day and Mother's Day.

Part 5

WHAT ARE AMISH COURTSHIP AND WEDDINGS LIKE?

What is *Rumspringa*? Is it true that all Amish teenagers leave home for a year to be "English"?

Are Amish marriages arranged? What is an Amish wedding like?

What is Rumspringa? *Is it true that all Amish teenagers leave home for a year to be "English"?*

At age sixteen or seventeen, depending on the church community, Amish girls and boys join the "youngie" or "young folk." They will likely stay with the young folk until marriage, a period of time also known as the "running around years" or *Rumspringa* (literally "running around"). Rumspringa varies from one Amish group to another but it rarely involves young Amish teenagers leaving home to be English (non-Amish) for a year.[1] It is a time of exploration and decision-making within the context of the church community. During this period, each Amish young person makes the two most important decisions of his or her lifetime: whether to join the Amish church through baptism and whom to take as a spouse.

Up until Rumspringa, the most important influence on an Amish young person is the family. Joining the young folk means that Amish youth are engaging in more activities with others their own age, away from direct parental oversight. The primary activity of young folk groups everywhere is the hymn singing that happens after supper on church Sunday evenings. Young folk gather at the home where services were held earlier that day and they sing hymns. The most traditional Amish young folk sing German songs while those in more progressive communities sing English songs, many of which would be familiar to anyone who has attended a Protestant church or Bible camp.

Rumspringa is a time for Amish dating. When the singing is over, a young man arranges to take a young girl home. This is normally what constitutes a date among the Amish. Once at the girl's home, the young man may stay and talk, either in the family kitchen or living room or in the girl's room, depending on the traditions of the church community.

Because daily activities are gendered, with young girls and boys working or socializing together rather than in mixed-sex groups, young men and young women spend little time together in mixed groups. Even at young folks' gatherings, girls sit separately, with couples pairing off for dates only at the end of the gathering. The conversation at home after the singing will likely be a couple's first chance to get to really know each other, even though they likely will have known each other their whole lives and may even have gone to school together. Further, until they marry, their dates will be the only time they spend alone together until they decide to marry and are "published," meaning that their engagement is announced in church.

In the most conservative communities, each church district has its own young folk group. It is only at larger gatherings, such as weddings or funerals or on trips with family, that young people encounter others beyond their particular district. At the other extreme are communities in which young folk groups will bring together young men and women from different church districts, and teens must choose which group they will join. In Lancaster County, for example, young folk groups or "gangs," with names like "Broncos" and "Swans," present teens with a choice between groups that engage in more traditional activities and those that push the limits of acceptable Amish behavior. While horse and buggy are still the primary means of transportation, young men may drive cars or trucks, while girls ride along. In such communities, girls may wear dresses that are shorter and more brightly colored than the Ordnung allows. They may even occasionally "dress English," meaning they wear non-Amish clothing when they are away from the family. Amish young folk activities in these progressive communities are more likely to include alcohol, smoking, and dancing. Nevertheless, even these young people live at home with their parents, help with chores, and go to church with their families.

In between the two extremes are Amish young people who spend their Rumspringa years dressing much like their parents, gathering to play volleyball or softball before the singing starts, and going as a group to help others or to sing to elderly church members. These groups often enjoy pizza parties, barbecues, and get-togethers with other young folk.

Roughly 85 percent of Amish young people join the church through baptism. Once Amish young men and women take this step, they must obey the local Ordnung. This means that there is usually a mix of baptized and not-yet-baptized men and women in every young folk gathering. When a young person becomes a church member and nears the age of twenty-one, the community begins to look for signs that a marriage is at hand.

Amish marriages are not arranged. Traditionally, young people keep their dating secret. This is still the goal among the most traditional Amish, who do not sanction young couples being seen together in public until their engagement has been announced in church. Once a couple has been "published," however, then all talk is of marriage. For the couple, this is the end of their Rumspringa.

Are Amish marriages arranged? What is an Amish wedding like?

Amish marriages are not arranged. Nevertheless, because marriage sets the stage for young people to have families and ensure the survival of the church community, parents and ministers do their best to ensure that couples start out strong in the ways of their faith.

It is traditional for a young man to ask a young woman for her hand, but her agreement is not all he needs. After she says yes, the young man must ask his deacon or another minister to act on his behalf and visit the young woman's parents to see if they will agree to the marriage. If they agree, the deacon goes to the bishop, who makes sure that all has been properly done. Only then can the upcoming marriage be "published," or announced in church. The couple is then officially engaged.

Until a couple is published, their courtship remains secret, a closely guarded one in more conservative communities and an often obvious one in more progressive groups. Certainly other members of their young folk group know about it, as do their parents, but others generally do not ask if they have "set a date."

In this and in many other ways, Amish weddings follow a pattern set long ago. The bride and groom must both be baptized before they can be married, and the ministers as well as the parents must approve of the match. The couple then enters into marriage with the support of their church community.

Even though the church community has not openly discussed whether a particular couple is likely to marry, if both the young man and woman are baptized, everyone eagerly awaits the announcement in church. Traditionally, Amish weddings have taken place in winter, after the harvest is over and the weather is cold enough to preserve the enormous amounts of food prepared for the wedding. In Lancaster County, the oldest Amish settlement in North America, the traditional wedding season lasts from September to December. Yet as the Amish population has grown, the wedding season has extended well into the spring. Further, as the Amish have moved into non-farming jobs and adopted refrigeration, weddings have begun to occur year-round. Today many Amish brides, like their non-Amish counterparts, look forward to a June wedding.

Weddings are usually held on Tuesdays and Thursdays. This gives the bride and her family time to prepare the food and ready the home. No work is done on Sunday, of course, and the family hopes to have everything put away by the Sunday following the wedding. In many communities a neighbor will host the wedding church service, and guests go to the bride's home for a meal following the service. In some communities, however, the bride's family hosts both the church service and meal, often building a large, temporary addition to the family home to hold all the guests.

The actual marriage ceremony itself takes place at the end of a normal church service, during which ministers traditionally draw on passages from the Old Testament and the book of Tobit. Found in the Apocrypha, the book of Tobit is used to emphasize the unbreakable holy bond created by marriage and the importance of this bond, for the couple and the entire church community. While the congregation sings, the bride and groom meet privately with the ministers for advice and blessings before they take their vows. Then, in front of family and friends, the bride and groom each promise to care for the other as befits a Christian spouse and to remain faithful until separated by death.[2] The bishop then prays for the couple and other clergy offer blessings. Finally, the couple and the congregation kneel in a closing prayer. Then the fun begins.

Weddings are large, usually involving anywhere from 200 to 1,000 guests. The bride's family is responsible for putting on the wedding. They will serve a large noon meal after the service, a large supper, snacks, and a midnight feast for the young folks. Although some families purchase baked goods, none of the meal is catered. This means that, in addition to inviting guests, the bride and groom must also ask some friends and family to serve as helpers. For example, they need cooks to prepare the large noon meal after the service, the supper, and the snacks. Usually aunts or married sisters of the bride and groom are invited for this job. Young men serve as "hostlers" to help with parking, and young girls serve as "table waiters" for the meals. For these tasks, the couple generally chooses friends from the young folk. Finally, the couple chooses their "side sitters," meaning couples who will stand with them during the marriage ceremony and sit with them at the *Eck* or corner table for the wedding feast. Traditionally, the side sitters are unmarried, and the bride and groom may take the opportunity to do some matchmaking.

The day of the wedding is a busy one. The bride's family often has the tables set in advance. Some communities have access to "wedding trailers" that come stocked with dishes, silverware, and pots and pans, but these must be reserved long in advance for the wedding season. In smaller, more conservative communities without such wedding supply businesses the bride borrows dishes, silverware, and cooking utensils from friends and neighbors. When guests arrive for the meal, they may find tables set with a variety of dishes. Whether the dishes are borrowed or rented, no table is set more nicely than the Eck, where the newlyweds sit between their side sitters. Just as the table is well-dressed, the bride and groom also have new outfits that they will likely wear to church for many Sundays to come. From their vantage point in the corner, the bridal party can see all the festivities.

After the meal, the cooks and table waiters clean up and begin preparing the evening supper, the men sing, and the children play. The newlyweds, along with their side sitters and other young folk, go to the bride's bedroom to open wedding gifts.

For families and married couples, the wedding festivities end with supper. The young folk stay late and supper is only the beginning of an evening of socializing and singing. But first they must go in to eat, which can be a stressful time for the unmarried youth, for young men and women go in to eat in pairs. In some communities, the men choose their partners. In others, the bride and groom take away some of the stress by pairing up the young folk themselves, a bit of matchmaking that helps to lay the groundwork for more wedding celebrations.

The day after the wedding, the newlyweds pitch in to help clean up. They often live with the bride's parents for a while until they can set up housekeeping on their own. Generally, the newlyweds will live near at least one set of parents. When they move into their new home, they will have furniture gifted from their parents, a variety of new housewares from friends and extended family, and a wealth of good wishes as they take their place in the church community.

Part 6

WHAT IS LIFE LIKE FOR AMISH ADULTS?

Are Amish women really submissive?

What kind of work do Amish men and women do?

What happens when Amish people age?

Are there Amish retirement communities?

What are Amish funerals like?

Are Amish women really submissive?

To determine if Amish women are submissive depends a lot on how one defines "submission." If you think it means that women must, without question, do everything their husbands (or men in general) tell them to, then the answer is a resounding "No!" Further, if you think it means that only women are submissive and that they have no right to speak up, then the answer is again a resounding "No!"

It is more accurate to say that Amish men and women have particular roles to play. When I asked one Amish woman about submission, she replied, "A husband and wife submit to each other and work together to make things work. Submission is really about talking. He has to submit too."

The Amish understanding of submission reflects the complicated place of gender within the church community. On the one hand, the Amish do assert that women should submit to their husbands, and they cite Ephesians 5:22-24, "Wives, submit yourselves unto your own husbands, as unto the Lord. For the husband is the head of the wife, even as Christ is the head of the church . . . Therefore as the church is subject unto Christ, so let the wives be to their own husbands in every thing."

Nevertheless, for the Amish, this hierarchy requires submission at all levels. While women submit to men, men must submit to God, and, in submitting, men must act in a particular way toward women. The Amish point to Ephesians 5:25, which commands husbands to "love your wives, even as Christ also loved the church, and gave himself for it."

The idea of a strict hierarchical relationship between men and women is further complicated when thinking of the church as the body of Christ, a body in which there is no male or female (1 Corinthians 12:12-27). Although only men can be ministers, women and men together decide when a new minister is needed and select candidates. In addition, women are responsible with men for obeying the Ordnung. Twice a year, men and women together must agree to the Ordnung, for only when all church members are in accord can communion be held. This means that women play an active role in informal debates and discussions within the church community that constrain the exercise of formal power.

In Amish life, the hierarchy that places men in authority over women operates in overtly religious contexts, as well as when the church community confronts the "English" or public world. As one researcher of Amish life put it, Amish husbands and wives "are to be as individuals to one another, and of one mind to all others." Therefore "the public 'stance' of the Amish family is one of wifely submission and obedience; in private and in practice, the family functions relatively democratically with important decisions . . . generally being made jointly (often with additional input from the extended family)."[1]

What kind of work do Amish men and women do?

The kind of work Amish men and women do depends on the type of community in which they live.

Traditionally, Amish women are responsible for taking care of the home, preparing meals, doing laundry, keeping the garden, and generally all things domestic. Amish men are responsible for work outside the home. Daughters help mothers, and sons help fathers. Yet this seemingly clear-cut division of labor has never been absolute. Men and boys have always helped with so-called "women's work" and vice versa. Men and women have together contributed to the economic health of the family and church community. While many men and boys continue to work as carpenters, furniture makers, and farmers, some work on assembly lines building everything from airplane interiors to parts for recreational vehicles. Women and girls continue to quilt, garden, sew clothes, and teach in Amish schools, but they may also be found working in offices, serving food in restaurants, and running their own businesses.

In traditional Amish farming communities, while men and women generally have distinct roles and responsibilities, they often work together, along with children and perhaps grandparents. While husband and sons take care of the planting, harvest the crops, and tend the livestock, wife and daughters take care of the home and meals, do the laundry and sew clothes, and tend the household garden. Both men and women are at home to help each other, and the entire family works together when necessary. In more conservative communities, children under the age of twenty-one are often employed within the church community as hired hands, schoolteachers, or household help. These young adults contribute their wages to the household income.

Other Amish church communities have turned to entrepreneurship, encouraging home-based, Amish-owned businesses. They have adopted and adapted technology to compete in a broader marketplace. Nowadays Amish business owners produce and market a variety of products, including solar panels, furniture, popcorn, and stoves, to consumers across North America. Both men and women have established commercial enterprises. For example, women now make up at least 15 percent of all Amish businessowners in Lancaster County.[2] In such communities, young people continue to work with their parents, boys entering their father's construction business, for example, or girls helping their mother with craft production or baking.

Gender influences who gets access to work outside the home. Simply put, men and unmarried girls have more opportunity to seek employment in the wider community. Married women, particularly if they have children, are expected to keep house and prepare meals. Nevertheless, married women continue to contribute to the economic well-being of their families and church community. Many women establish home-based businesses, putting traditional skills to work to earn an income. For example, even in the most conservative Amish church communities, women sell produce, crafts, and baked goods. Women are also likely to establish businesses that serve their Amish neighbors, including bulk food or dry goods stores.

What happens when Amish people age?

The Amish ideal is to grow old in the church community among family and friends. When an Amish couple decides to retire, they usually sell their farm or business to one of their children and move into a *Dawdyhaus*, which is a small house or apartment adjacent to the home of one of their married offspring. *Dawdies* means grandparents in Pennsylvania Dutch, and *Dawdyhaus* is a "grandparents' house." In the Dawdyhaus, the couple continue to do just about everything they did before "retiring." They keep house and assist some with the farm work. They no longer host church in their own home, but otherwise they remain active church members.

The Amish do not participate in the United States Social Security system. After older people move into a Dawdyhaus, they live on the proceeds of the sale of their farm or business. They may also hold an auction of their surplus furniture and other goods, with the money going to their retirement nest egg. Some may continue to generate income through a home business or part-time work. Generally, grandchildren may help run errands and married children take turns visiting to help with chores and upkeep. For example, many retired couples enjoy fall gatherings with their married children who work together to fill their woodhouse.

When an elderly parent can no longer take care of himself or herself, then children or grandchildren assume responsibility for their care. After a spouse has passed away and the surviving parent can no longer cope alone, the married children will take turns staying with the parent in the Dawdyhaus or caring for him or her in their own homes.

Are there Amish retirement communities?

For the majority of elderly Amish, retirement does not mean moving to a separate community. It means living independently in one's own home in close proximity to family, enjoying daily interaction with children and grandchildren, and participating actively in the church community.

In more conservative Amish communities, it also means working with children and grandchildren as long as one is able. Particularly in farming communities, the wisdom of older people is prized, and their knowledge and skills can be handed down to younger generations, who learn to do the same kind of work their parents and grandparents did by laboring alongside them.

As Amish church communities have shifted from farming to entrepreneurship and working for others, however, work skills have become more specialized. Today many Amish have jobs at sites distant from the family home. As a result, children may no longer gain the knowledge they need to earn a living by working with their parents and grandparents, and grandparents no longer count on being active in the work lives of their grandchildren. Further, a growing dependence on wage labor or entrepreneurship means more disposable income. No longer needed at home and with more money at hand, older, more progressive Amish, like their non-Amish counterparts, head south for the winter.

The Pinecraft community on the outskirts of Sarasota, Florida, is the closest thing to a retirement community in the Amish world. Established in the late 1920s, Pinecraft welcomes nearly 4,000 snowbirds a week during January and February, with an average of ten busloads of mostly older Amish arriving each week. While there is a year-round Amish church community in Pinecraft, most of its members live elsewhere much of the year.[3]

The Pinecraft settlement has been described as being in "Ordnung limbo" since most who stay there are away from their own church communities. As a result, the Amish in Pinecraft enjoy a variety of things that would not be permitted in their own homes, including microwaves, air conditioning, and motorized carts. Secure in the understanding that what happens in Pinecraft stays in Pinecraft, these Amish snowbirds live in retirement quite differently from their more conservative counterparts, who could not afford winter homes or imagine being so distant from their families and church communities for an extended time.

What are Amish funerals like?

For the Amish, an ideal death occurs at home with family and friends. A dying church member is visited by relatives and friends. Together, they spend time catching up, talking quietly of old times, shared experiences, and personal events. Members of the community come to take over chores so that family members can catch up with sleep and spend time with their loved one. The Amish welcome and use hospice services, but it is the church community upon which the family truly depends.

After death, neighbors spread the word, and friends of the family ensure that those in other communities are informed of the name and age of the deceased and the time and place of the funeral. All Amish communities keep lists of non-Amish phone numbers for such occasions, and non-Amish friends and neighbors are pressed into service to make the calls or to carry the "death message." Once notified, those in distant settlements begin packing immediately, making arrangements to get to a bus or to hire a driver and, if necessary, to get someone to take over chores or care for small children. When the deceased is elderly and death is expected, families prepare in advance, and attendance at the funeral is large. An unexpected or sudden death means family and friends have to hurry to make arrangements, and not everyone can attend who would like to.

There are no flowers at an Amish funeral, and the service itself takes place in the home of the deceased or a close relative. (If the deceased is well-known, the funeral service may be held simultaneously in several places. For example, the funeral sermon of one elderly bishop was preached in three different homes.) The oldest married couple in the congregation who are not part of the family supervise the many community members who arrive to clean the house, take over chores, and do the cooking for the bereaved family. Men set up benches in the home so that visitors who come to mourn will have a place to sit as they hold vigil until the funeral. In most communities, a local funeral home will prepare the body and return it to the home for the funeral. However, church members wash and dress the body in the most conservative communities. A member of the community makes the plain wooden coffin in which the deceased will be buried.

Once the body has been prepared, it is laid out in a side room for visitors to come and pay their respects. As mourners enter the main room, they shake hands with those already there. Then, at various times during the day, those who have come to mourn are invited to enter the room where the deceased is laid out to see the body and to offer their respects. Even the youngest children are taken in to see the body, learning early that death is a natural part of life.

On the day of the funeral, the benches are arranged as for a regular church service, except that the benches in the main room are set up so that the coffin can be put on trestles in the middle of the room and family members can sit around it. A minister from the deceased's own church usually preaches the main sermon but visiting ministers may also be involved in the service. There is no eulogy. While the deceased's life will be mentioned, the focus of the sermon will be about preparing for the inevitability of death. If the funeral is for an infant or a young child, then the minister will emphasize the child's innocence and the sure welcome that awaits the child in heaven.

There is no singing at an Amish funeral service. After the preaching and a prayer, a minister reads the deceased's obituary, and the congregation files past the coffin to say a last farewell before the lid is closed and nailed shut. Then, after a final prayer, the coffin is put on a wagon to be taken to the cemetery. Church members walk or follow in their buggies to the cemetery, where men from the church community have already dug the grave.

Most Amish cemeteries are on land donated by a member of the church community. At the graveside, family and friends of all ages gather as the coffin is put into the ground, a hymn is read rather than sung, and the grave filled in. Again, there are no flowers. Many will then go back to the home of the deceased to share a meal provided by women in the church community.

Later, the family will put up a gravestone, one likely made by another community member. In some communities, the grave marker is made of wood and will eventually disappear. Family members will visit the grave in the following years but they will not bring flowers.

In joining to mourn, the Amish reinforce their understanding of life in this world as temporary, a passage to eternal life in the next. The thought that their loved one is now free of the suffering of worldly existence comforts Amish mourners.

Part 7

WHAT WILL AMISH LIFE BE LIKE IN THE FUTURE?

What problems do the Amish face?
What holds Amish communities together?

What problems do the Amish face?

The Amish rely on the non-Amish world. They are not self-sufficient and rely on interacting with non-Amish people when they shop, visit a doctor or hospital, or deposit money in a bank. They also sell produce and goods to non-Amish customers. Many work for non-Amish employers. As the non-Amish world becomes more technological, more global, and more digital, the Amish find themselves forced to change as well.

Until the twentieth century, most Amish were farmers and used technology similar to that of their non-Amish neighbors. Amish life was seasonal, driven by the cycle of farming and food preservation. While the Amish lacked electricity, telephones, indoor plumbing, automobiles, and luxury items such as radios, so did their rural non-Amish neighbors. Then mainstream American society changed. Non-Amish farmers began to mechanize production with tractors to plow more and more acreage while Amish farmers found it harder to find affordable farmland and to compete with their neighbors for access to markets.

In the mid-twentieth century, nearly all Amish families earned their living by farming. Today, the percentage of those financially dependent on agriculture is as low as 17 percent in the Holmes County area of Ohio—the nation's largest Amish settlement. In Geauga County, Ohio, the number of Amish still farming was down to 7 percent, and in the state of Delaware the number was down to 25 percent. Roughly 25 percent of the families in the large Elkhart-Lagrange, Indiana, Amish settlement were still farming in 1995. But by 2002, only 17 percent were.[1]

Seeking to sustain themselves economically, Amish church communities have tended to follow one of three paths. Some have fostered entrepreneurship within the community, encouraging church members to establish manufacturing, service, and retail businesses. These communities have also permitted greater and varied interaction with the non-Amish marketplace so that Amish businesses can compete and succeed. For example, in Lancaster County, Pennsylvania, one can find Amish businesses that market diverse products (e.g., popcorn, wood-burning stoves, solar panels, hydroponically grown lettuce) to consumers across North America. In these entrepreneurial communities, both men and women have become business owners. Young people are still likely to grow up working for and with their parents, or other members of the church community. Yet labor is no longer like it was on small family farms, when all joined together to accomplish the larger tasks of harvest and food preservation.

Other Amish church communities have approved of church members working for non-Amish employers. Church members have gone to work on assembly lines, in the hospitality trade, and for other types of local non-Amish employers. Working on assembly lines, today's Amish have helped build such diverse products as cabinets for corporate jets, garage doors, and luxury motor homes. Amish may also work as waitstaff and cooks in restaurants and clerks in stores. As members of the church community have gone to work away from home, Amish men and women have been affected differently. For example, since married women with children are generally expected to care for children and the home, it is more often the husband who works outside the community. Further, children can no longer work alongside older family members, so they must rely more on formal and vocational education. In such communities, it has become more important for Amish schools to prepare children for a life in which they will spend a large amount of time outside the church community.

The most conservative Amish have clung to farming, and they have rejected or severely limited the use of technology. When they can no longer find enough farmland for married children in one location, their response has been to move, establishing new settlements in regions where cheap, available farmland allows them to continue their agrarian way of life. Since the mid-twentieth century, conservative Amish have established communities in Maine, Vermont, Montana, and Wyoming. Since 2000, Amish in Canada have left Ontario, where they first settled in the early nineteenth century, moving west to Manitoba and east to Prince Edward Island and New Brunswick. In these conservative communities, women and men may take responsibility for different tasks but they help each other. Children learn from parents and grandparents by working with them on a variety of tasks. Important lessons continue to be learned in shared labor rather than in the schoolhouse.

Each approach to dealing with the changing non-Amish world poses challenges. Families in entrepreneurial communities and families who work for non-Amish employers generally have greater financial resources than farming families. A reliable cash income means that families can purchase goods that their farming grandparents once produced themselves or did without. In other words, moving away from a self-sufficient, agrarian economy allows for greater personal wealth and contributes to the development of a consumer culture. Such families are then less tied to neighbors and live in much closer contact with mainstream society, which emphasizes the acquisition of personal goods and leisure time over work. There may even be time and money for vacations away from the church community and even snow-birding vacations to Florida (see page 93).

When church members enter into regular business or work arrangements with those outside the church community, they may begin to challenge traditional notions of what it means to be separate from the world. Needing to compete more directly with non-Amish businesses and labor, Amish in these settings may even question the extent to which the Ordnung should govern daily lives, a direct challenge to the ties that bind the church community together.

On the other hand, their agrarian Amish counterparts continue to work together across generational and gender lines, joining with neighbors to accomplish larger tasks such as harvesting. Yet these Amish often live at a subsistence level in a world in which they find it increasingly difficult to market goods, get information, and navigate mainstream society. They are challenged to order goods when manufacturers no longer supply catalogs, expecting customers to search online. Even as they attempt to keep the old ways of working and earning a living, they find they must change. To bring in extra cash, many Amish sell crafts at small farm stands and have been learning to make old things in new ways to meet customers' demand. For example, Amish women make quilts, pot holders, and other items for the tourist market using colors and types of fabric not permitted in their own homes. Amish shed makers now construct tiny houses for the non-Amish market, and harness makers construct fancy bridles for non-Amish show horses.

Further, as conservative Amish establish new settlements to maintain their agrarian way of life, they encounter a non-Amish world that is not used to their way of life. In a number of states, the Amish have come into conflict with their non-Amish neighbors, as well as local and state authorities, over requirements that homes be built with sewers and that buggies carry the slow-moving vehicle triangle, for example. Changing notions of childhood and children working have also put pressure on Amish families to restrict the kind of work children do. This is particularly true in the most conservative church communities, where children are more likely to work with parents in a variety of settings (e.g., sawmills) that secular society sees as particularly dangerous. Despite an Amish willingness to work out compromises with secular authorities, the conservative Amish, who establish new settlements so that they can maintain their traditions, resist change to the Ordnungs.

As the Amish accept new ways of earning a living and supporting their families, they redraw the lines that separate the church community from the world, so innovation and change in the non-Amish world will continue to affect Amish life. As more and more American business is conducted online, Amish church communities that resist electricity, computers, and the internet will be increasingly isolated from their mainstream neighbors. Or they will be increasingly dependent on them for access to goods and services.

What holds Amish communities together?

The Amish world is far more diverse than it was a hundred years ago. This has led some to question what it is that holds the Amish world together. The simple answer is their faith.

Like their Anabaptist ancestors, today's Amish devote their lives to the service of God and to following Christ's example regardless of the personal cost. The Lord's Prayer says, "thy will be done" (Matthew 6:10) and the Amish still strive to put Christ's teachings into practice in their daily lives.

Further, the Amish understand earthly life as just a prelude to eternal life—if one is worthy. Like their forebears, they hold fast to the injunction in Romans 12:2 to remain "not conformed" to the world. They point to James 4:4, which asks, "Know ye not that the friendship of the world is enmity with God?" In choosing to be Amish, they choose to live lives unlike those of their "English" neighbors. They express their faith in the clothes they put on in the morning, the food they eat, the furniture they use in their homes, the restrictions they place around technology, and their practices of education and childrearing.

And these choices continue to bring them into conflict.

Conflict reinforces faith. Identifying with their persecuted forebears, the Amish accept that the sincere practice of their faith will certainly make daily life more difficult, and may lead to conflict with earthly authorities. They point out that Christ was persecuted, and so those who follow Christ's example should expect no less.

Ironically, even as the Amish interact with the secular world, they reject it. And by rejecting it, they define themselves. Even as Amish church communities innovate or church members become more engaged in the mainstream economy, the Amish are likely to highlight cultural and religious differences by drawing an ever sharper line between Amish ways and worldly ones. In making a baptismal vow and becoming a member of an Amish church community, each Amish person makes an active commitment to being different and living differently from those in the non-Amish world. Those who are unwilling or unable to make the commitment leave the church.

In many respects, the Amish are always in church, for they live their lives according to the Ordnung of their church community. Thus, they confront daily the boundary between the Amish and non-Amish worlds, and the Amish world remains a visible alternative to modern society. According to one popular book on the Amish, "There is no other way to explain why so many tens of thousands stay, why in fact the communities are growing in number."[2]

The Amish remain cohesive by defining themselves against the norms established by mainstream society. As the Amish interact with the secular world, they reject it, and, in doing so, thrive.

SOURCES CITED

Baecher, R. "Research Note: The 'Patriarche' of Sainte-Marie-aux-Mines," *Mennonite Quarterly Review* 74 (2000): 151–152.

Crowley, W. K. "Old Order Amish Settlement: Diffusion and Growth." *Annals of the Association of American Geographers* 68, no. 2 (1978): 249–264.

Furlong, S. M. *Why I left the Amish: A Memoir*. East Lansing: Michigan State University Press, 2011.

Good, M., and P. Good. *20 Most Asked Questions about the Amish and Mennonites*. Intercourse, PA: Good Books, 1995.

Graber, O. A. "Gleanings from Yesterday." *Die Botschaft*, April 6, 1998.

Guth, H. *Amish Mennonites in Germany: Their Congregations, The Estates Where They Lived, Their Families*. Metamora, IL: Illinois Mennonite Historical and Genealogical Society, 1995.

Hostetler, J. A. *Amish Society*. 4th ed. Baltimore: Johns Hopkins University Press, 1993.

Huntington, G. E. "Occupational Opportunities for Old Order Amish Women." *Pennsylvania Folklife* 43, no.3 (1994): 115-120.

———. "Persistence and Change in Amish Education." In *The Amish Struggle with Modernity*, edited by D. B. Kraybill and M. A. Olshan, 77-95. Hanover, NY: University Press of New England, 1994.

Johnson-Weiner, K. M. *New York Amish: Life in the Plain Communities of the Empire State*. 2nd ed. Ithaca, NY: Cornell University Press, 2017.

————. *Train Up a Child: Old Order Amish and Mennonite Schools.* Baltimore: Johns Hopkins University Press, 2007.

Keim, A. N. *Compulsory Education and the Amish: The Right Not to Be Modern.* Boston: Beacon Press, 1975.

Kraybill, D. B., K. M. Johnson-Weiner, and S. M. Nolt. *The Amish.* Baltimore: Johns Hopkins University Press, 2013.

Nolt, S. M. *A History of the Amish.* 3rd ed. New York: Good Books, 2015.

Nolt, S. M., and T. J. Meyers. *Plain Diversity: Amish Cultures and Identities.* Baltimore: Johns Hopkins University Press, 2007.

Stoll, J. "German and English." *The Blackboard Bulletin*, May 1969, 207-209.

Stoltzfus, G. M. *Mennonites of the Ohio and Eastern Conference from the Colonial Period in Pennsylvania to 1968.* Scottdale, PA: Herald Press, 1969.

Wagler, I. *Growing Up Amish.* Carol Stream, IL: Tyndale House Publishers, 2011.

Wesner, E. *Success Made Simple: An Inside Look at Why Amish Businesses Thrive.* San Francisco: Jossey-Bass, 2010.

FOR FURTHER READING

For More about the Amish

Cates, J. A. *Serving the Amish: A Cultural Guide for Professionals.* Baltimore: Johns Hopkins University Press, 2014.

Hostetler, J. A. *Amish Roots: A Treasury of History, Wisdom, and Lore.* Baltimore: Johns Hopkins University Press, 1989.

Igou, B. *Amish Voices: A Collection of Amish Writings.* Harrisonburg, VA: Herald Press, 2019.

Kraybill, D. B., ed. *The Amish and the State.* 2nd ed. Baltimore: Johns Hopkins University Press, 2003.

———. *The Riddle of Amish Culture.* Rev. ed. Baltimore: Johns Hopkins University Press, 2001.

———. *Simply Amish: An Essential Guide.* Harrisonburg, VA: Herald Press, 2018.

Kraybill, D. B., and S. M. Nolt. *Amish Enterprise: From Plows to Profits.* Rev. ed. Baltimore: Johns Hopkins University Press, 2004.

Kraybill, D. B., and M. Olshan, eds. *The Amish Struggle with Modernity.* Hanover, NH: University Press of New England, 1994.

Längin, B. G. *Plain and Amish: An Alternative to Modern Pessimism.* Scottdale, PA: Herald Press, 1994.

Umble, D. Zimmerman. *Holding the Line: The Telephone in Old Order Amish and Mennonite Life*. Baltimore: Johns Hopkins University Press, 1996.

Umble, D. Zimmerman and D. L. Weaver-Zercher. *The Amish and the Media*. Baltimore: Johns Hopkins University Press, 2008.

Weaver-Zercher, D. L. *The Amish in the American Imagination*. Baltimore: Johns Hopkins University Press, 2001.

Weaver-Zercher, V. *Thrill of the Chaste: The Allure of Amish Romance Novels*. Baltimore: Johns Hopkins University Press, 2013.

Amish in Different States

Clark, A. B. *This is Good Country: A History of the Amish of Delaware, 1915–1988*. Gordonville, PA: Gordonville Print Shop, 1989. (Delaware)

Huntington, G. E. *Amish in Michigan*. East Lansing: Michigan State University Press, 2001. (Michigan)

Hurst, C. E., and D. L. McConnell. *An Amish Paradox: Diversity and Change in the World's Largest Amish Community*. Baltimore: Johns Hopkins University Press, 2010. (Ohio, particularly the Holmes County area)

Johnson-Weiner, K. M. *New York Amish: Life in the Plain Communities of the Empire State*. 2nd ed. Ithaca, NY: Cornell University Press, 2017. (New York)

Kraybill, D. B. *The Riddle of Amish Culture*. Rev. ed. Baltimore: Johns Hopkins University Press, 2001. (Pennsylvania, particularly Lancaster County)

Meyers, T. J., and S. M. Nolt. *An Amish Patchwork: Indiana's Old Orders in the Modern World*. Bloomington, IN: Quarry Books, 2005. (Indiana)

Nolt, S. M., and T. J. Meyers. *Plain Diversity: Amish Cultures and Identities*. Baltimore: Johns Hopkins University Press, 2007. (Indiana)

Schwieder, E., and D. Schwieder. *A Peculiar People: Iowa's Old Order Amish*. Ames: The Iowa State University Press, 1975. (Iowa)

On Language

Brown, J. *Schwetz mol Deitsch! An Introductory Pennsylvania Dutch Course*. Millersville, PA: The Center for German-American Studies, 2009.

Hoover, A. B. *German Language: Cradle of Our Heritage*. Ephrata, PA: Muddy Creek Farm Library, 2018.

Louden, M. L. *Pennsylvania Dutch: The Story of an American Language*. Baltimore: Johns Hopkins University Press, 2016.

On Education

Dewalt, M. *Amish Education in the United States and Canada*. Lanham, MD: Rowman & Littlefield Education, 2006.

Fisher, S. E., and R. K. Stahl. *The Amish School*. Rev. ed. Intercourse, PA: Good Books, 1997.

Johnson-Weiner, K. M. *Train Up a Child: Old Order Amish and Mennonite Schools*. Baltimore: Johns Hopkins University Press, 2007.

On Amish Young People

Mackall, J. *Plain Secrets: An Outsider among the Amish*. Boston: Beacon Press, 2007.

Shachtman, T. *Rumspringa*. New York: North Point Press, 2006.

Stevick, R. *Growing Up Amish: The Teenage Years*. 2nd ed. Baltimore: Johns Hopkins University Press, 2014.

On Amish Women

Johnson-Weiner, K. M. *The Lives of Amish Women*. Baltimore: Johns Hopkins University Press, 2020.

Schmidt, K. D., D. Zimmerman Umble, and S. D. Reschly, eds. *Strangers at Home: Amish and Mennonite Women in History*. Baltimore: Johns Hopkins University Press, 2002.

Stevick, P. *Beyond the Plain and Simple: A Patchwork of Amish Lives*. Kent, OH: The Kent State University Press, 2006.

Stoltzfus, L. *Amish Women: Lives and Stories*. Intercourse, PA: Good Books, 1994.

Yoder, L. *My Life as an Amish Wife*. Eugene, OR: Harvest House Publishers, 2015.

Amish Memoir

Beachy, Loren. *Chasing the Amish Dream: My Life as a Young Amish Bachelor*. Harrisonburg, VA: Herald Press, 2014.

Jantzi, Marianne. *Simple Pleasures: Stories from My Life as an Amish Mother*. Harrisonburg, VA: Herald Press, 2016.

Miller, Marlene C. *Called to Be Amish: My Journey from Head Majorette to the Old Order*. Harrisonburg, VA: Herald Press, 2015.

ACKNOWLEDGMENTS

I am grateful to the many Amish people who have welcomed me into their homes and patiently answered my questions about their lives and their faith.

I also wish to thank Dr. Patricia Alden and Donna Smith-Raymond for taking time to read and comment on earlier drafts of this work. Their feedback was much appreciated. As always, I thank my husband and eager editor, Bruce, for his willingness to chop my work to bits. I'm a better writer for it.

Of course, I take full responsibility for any faults that remain.

NOTES

Part 1

1. The term *Anabaptist* was a pejorative label applied by supporters of the state church. Meaning "rebaptizers," it referred to those who rebaptized themselves as followers of the new church.
2. A confession is a statement of religious doctrine.
3. Robert Baecher, "Research Note: The 'Patriarche' of Sainte-Marie-aux-Mines," *Mennonite Quarterly Review* 74 (January 2000), 151–152.
4. John A. Hostetler, *Amish Society*, 4th ed. (Baltimore: Johns Hopkins University Press, 1993), 39.
5. W. K. Crowley, "Old Order Amish Settlement: Diffusion and Growth," *Annals of the Association of American Geographers* 68, no. 2: 249-264.
6. Today there are no Amish left in Europe from the original Amish congregations, congregations that, as John A. Hostetler put it, "retained the name and practices of the original group" (*Amish Society*, 66). The last such Amish congregation, the Amish church in Ixheim, Germany, merged with a neighboring Mennonite congregation in 1937. (Crowley, 1978; Hostetler, 1993: 66). Beachy Amish missionaries from North America have engaged in missionary work in Europe, establishing a number

of Beachy Amish congregations since the 1960s. A congregation was established in Ukraine in 2006. See Cory Anderson, "Beachy Amish Mennonite Fellowship," *Global Anabaptist Mennonite Encyclopedia Online* (May 2014), https://gameo.org/index .php?title=Beachy_Amish_Mennonite_Fellowship&oldid=162460.

7. O. A. Graber, "Gleanings from Yesterday," *Die Botschaft* (April 6, 1988), 17.

8. G. M. Stoltzfus, *Mennonites of the Ohio and Eastern Conference from the Colonial Period in Pennsylvania to 1968* (Scottdale, PA: Herald Press, 1969). Stoltzfus notes that forty of the seventy-two participants at the 1862 meeting were from Ohio. See p. 158.

9. These statistics are from "Amish Population, 2019," Young Center for Anabaptist and Pietist Studies, Elizabethtown College, http:// groups.etown.edu/amishstudies/statistics/population-2019/

Part 2

1. For more on Pennsylvania Dutch, see Mark Louden, *Pennsylvania Dutch: The Story of an American Language* (Baltimore: Johns Hopkins University Press, 2016) and Joshua Brown, *Schwetz mol Deitsch: An Introductory Pennsylvania Dutch Course* (Millersville, PA: The Center for German-American Studies, 2009).

2. Translations of German titles are from John A. Hostetler, *Amish Society*, 4th ed. (Baltimore, MD: Johns Hopkins University Press, 1993), 106.

3. Because they allow the milk to be refrigerated (in the most conservative communities, such tanks are owned by the dairy companies), bulk milk tanks make it possible for the Amish to ship Grade A milk. When the Amish ship milk in cans, it can only be sold to cheese factories.

4. Hostetler, *Amish Society*, 225.

5. In his book *Compulsory Education and the Amish* (Boston: Beacon Press, 1975), A. N. Keim quotes Bishop David O. Treyer of Ohio, who, writing in 1870, argued that "All Christian churches must be fenced-in (*um zäunt*) with rules and regulations which are based and grounded on God's Word. For without such a spiritual fence no church can long survive. Where no Christian 'Ordnung' exists, God cannot be served" (10).

6. D.B. Kraybill, K. M. Johnson-Weiner, and S. Nolt, *The Amish* (Baltimore: Johns Hopkins University Press, 2013), 161.

7. K. M. Johnson-Weiner, *New York Amish* (Ithaca, NY: Cornell University Press, 2017), 48. See also Kraybill et al., *The Amish*, 165–168.
8. Numerous Bible verses reinforce this commandment. See especially Deuteronomy 5:16 and Ephesians 6:2-3.
9. For example, in his memoir *Growing Up Amish* (Carol Stream, IL: Tyndale House Publishers, 2011), Ira Wagler recounts leaving home four times before he finally left for good at age twenty-six and joined a Mennonite church.
10. Kraybill, Johnson-Weiner, and Nolt, *The Amish*, 162–165.
11. Saloma Miller Furlong, for example, points to both abuse in her immediate family and to a lack of support in her church community to explain why she left the Amish. S. M. Furlong, *Why I Left the Amish: A Memoir* (East Lansing: Michigan State University Press, 2011).
12. Charles E. Hurst and David L. McConnell, *An Amish Paradox: Diversity and Change in the World's Largest Amish Community* (Baltimore: John Hopkins University Press, 2010), 84–85.

Part 3

1. English, as one Amish person put it, is the language "we associate with the business world, society, and worldliness. . . . English in a sense represents everything outside our church and community . . ." Joseph Stoll, "German and English," *The Blackboard Bulletin*, May 1969, 207–209.
2. See D.B. Kraybill, K. M. Johnson-Weiner, and S. Nolt, *The Amish* (Baltimore: Johns Hopkins University Press, 2013), 314.
3. For more on this, see Kraybill, Johnson-Weiner, Nolt, *The Amish*, 314–318
4. Changes in the way in which Amish men and women work together both influence and result from broader economic and social change in the church community. They are part of a growing diversity within the Amish world. The impact of such changes on the lives of Amish women is considered in depth in K. M. Johnson-Weiner, *The Lives of Amish Women* (Johns Hopkins University Press, 2020). See also Kraybill, Johnson-Weiner, and Nolt, *The Amish*.
5. Dordrecht Confession, Article 13, *Mennonite Confession of Faith*, 7th printing (Crockett, KY: Rod and Staff Publishers, 1989), 76.
6. See Kraybill, Johnson-Weiner, and Nolt, *The Amish*, 361–362.

7. *1001 Questions and Answers on the Christian Life* (Aylmer, ON: Pathway, 1992), 158.

8. For more on beards, see http://gameo.org/index.php?title=Beard.

9. Hermann Guth, *Amish Mennonites in Germany: Their Congregations, the Estates Where They Lived, Their Families* (Metamora, IL: Illinois Mennonite Historical and Genealogical Society, 1995), 3.

10. Sumptuary laws are laws intended to regulate consumption. In Europe after the Reformation, such laws were designed to enforce class and gender distinctions in dress.

11. S. M. Nolt, *A History of the Amish* (New York: Good Books, 2015) 49.

Part 4

1. See K. M. Johnson-Weiner, *Train Up a Child* (Baltimore: Johns Hopkins University Press, 2007), 7; D.B. Kraybill, K. M. Johnson-Weiner, and S. Nolt, *The Amish* (Baltimore: Johns Hopkins University Press, 2013), 254–255.

2. A. N. Keim, *Compulsory Education and the Amish: The Right Not to Be Modern* (Boston: Beacon Press, 1975), 98.

3. G. E. Huntington, "Persistence and Change in Amish education," in in *The Amish Struggle with Modernity*, eds. D. B. Kraybill and M. A. Olshan (Hanover, NH: University Press of New England, 1994), 78.

4. For a good listing of Amish periodicals, see https://groups.etown .edu/amishstudies/resources/amish-publications/.

5. For a good description of Amish church services, see J. A. Hostetler, *Amish Society* (Baltimore: Johns Hopkins University Press, 1993), 210–219; also D.B. Kraybill, K. M. Johnson-Weiner, and S. Nolt, *The Amish* (Baltimore: Johns Hopkins University Press, 2013), chapter 5.

Part 5

1. Simply put, if an Amish young person were to leave home, then he or she would be unable to engage in the activities considered appropriate for this time. Various reality TV shows (e.g., *Amish in the City* or *Amish: Out of Order*) are scripted non-Amish productions, not windows into Amish reality. For more, see Claire J. Harris, "I Worked for an Amish Reality TV Show," *Gen,* (August 7, 2019), https://gen.medium.com/i-worked-for-an-amish-reality-tv-show-1d29f0e384ba. See also "The Ugly

Reality Behind Amish "Reality" TV," in "Amish Controversies," *Amish America* (August 16, 2019), https://amishamerica.com/ugly-behind-the-scenes-amish-reality-tv/.

2. *In Meiner Jugend: A Devotional Reader in German and English* (Aylmer, ON: Pathway Publishers, 2000) offers English translations of the wedding questions used in different communities. See pages 208–227.

Part 6

1. G. E. Huntington, "Occupational Opportunities for Old Order Amish Women," *Pennsylvania Folklife* 43, no. 3 (1994):115–120, 114.

2. See E. Wesner, *Success Made Simple: An Inside Look at Why Amish Businesses Thrive* (San Francisco: Jossey-Bass, 2010), 12. D. B. Kraybill et al., *The Amish* (Baltimore: Johns Hopkins University Press, 2013), 305.

3. See Kraybill et al., *The Amish*, 241–243, for more on the Pinecraft "snowbirds."

Part 7

1. S. M. Nolt and T. J. Meyers, *Plain Diversity* (Baltimore: Johns Hopkins University Press, 2007), 87.

2. Merle and Phyllis Good, *20 Most Asked Questions about the Amish and Mennonites* (Intercourse, PA: Good Books, 1995), 84.

THE AUTHOR

Karen Johnson-Weiner is coauthor of *The Amish* (with Donald B. Kraybill and Steven M. Nolt) and author of *Train Up a Child* and *New York Amish*. With degrees from Hope College, Michigan State, and McGill University, she is professor emerita of anthropology at SUNY Potsdam. Johnson-Weiner has studied and related to the Amish for more than thirty years.